Effective Fostering Panels

Sarah Borthwick with
Jenifer Lord

Published by CoramBAAF Adoption and Fostering
Academy
41 Brunswick Square
London WC1N 1AZ
www.corambaaf.org.uk

Coram Academy Limited, registered as a company
limited by guarantee in England and Wales number
9697712, part of the Coram group, charity number
312278.

© BAAF, 2003, 2007, 2011, 2015
Originally published by BAAF
This edition published by CoramBAAF
© CoramBAAF 2019

British Library Cataloguing in Publication Data
A catalogue record for this book is available from the
British Library

ISBN 978 1 910039 79 3

Designed and typeset by Helen Joubert Design
Printed in Great Britain by The Lavenham Press
All rights reserved. Except as permitted under
the Copyright, Designs and Patents Act 1988, this
publication may not be reproduced, stored in a
retrieval system, or transmitted in any form or by any
means, without the prior written permission
of the publishers.

The moral right of the authors has been asserted in
accordance with the Copyright, Designs and Patents
Act 1988.

 For the latest news on CoramBAAF titles and special offers, sign up to our
free publications bulletin at https://corambaaf.org.uk/subscribe.

Contents

Introduction	**1**
How this guide will help you	2
What this guide covers	2
Notes on terminology	3

1 Establishing a fostering panel — **4**
- Membership – the regulations — 4
- Membership – practice issues — 4
- Checks on panel members — 8
- Tenure — 9
- Panel membership agreement — 9
- Review of panel members — 10
- Fees for panel members — 11
- Quorum — 11
- Declaring an interest — 11
- Non-panel members — 11
- Sending information to panel members — 12
- Panel information leaflet and member profiles — 12
- Administration — 12
- Main administrative functions — 12
- Minutes — 13
- Fostering inspection — 14
- Remit of the panel — 14

2 Agency policy and practice issues — **15**
- Relevant legislation and guidance — 15
- Other relevant legislation and guidance — 16
- General policies and practice relating to fostering — 17
- Specific issues that panel members will need to consider — 17
- Contact — 21
- Allowances — 21
- Long-term fostering (permanence plan) — 22
- Short break carers — 22
- Concurrent or dually-approved carers — 22
- Fostering for Adoption — 22
- Annual review — 23
- Representations and complaints — 23

3 Children requiring foster care — **24**
- The needs of children — 24
- Child-focused service — 25
- Permanence plans for children — 25
- Remit of the panel in permanence planning — 26
- Information required in recommending permanent matches — 26

4 Considering the approval of foster carers — **27**
- The panel's legal functions — 27
- The panel's role: messages from Serious Case Reviews — 27
- Assessments of foster carers — 27
- Stage 1 — 27
- Checks and references — 27
- Stage 2 — 29
- Further checks and references — 29
- Brief reports — 30
- The full assessment report — 30
- Panel members' responsibilities — 31
- Attending the panel — 32
- Reaching a recommendation — 33
- Approvals – decision-making process — 34
- Qualifying determinations and representations – decision-making process — 35
- Range of fostering tasks — 36

5 Family and friends as foster carers (connected persons) — **37**
- Arrangements for the care of children — 37
- Immediate placement — 38
- Issues concerning family and friends as foster carers — 39

National Minimum Standards	39	Appendix 1: Introduction to Fostering Services: National Minimum Standards 2011	63
Age and health	39		
Convictions	39		
Smoking	40	Appendix 2: Training, Support and Development Standards	64
Child protection	40		
Views of the child	40	Appendix 3: Decision-making forms	66
Report to panel	41		

6 **Reviews and changes and terminations of approval** — 42

Legal functions — 42
Reviews of foster carers — 42
Change of approval — 44
Terminations of approval — 45
Terminations: the role of the panel — 46

7 **Monitoring and quality assurance** — 48

Monitoring — 48
Annual report — 48
Business meetings — 49
Training — 49

Conclusion — 50

References — 51

Glossary — 54

Useful organisations — 59

Appendix 4: Job descriptions and person specifications for central list/panel members and panel Chair — 70

Appendix 5: Interview questions for central list/panel members and panel Chair — 74

Appendix 6: Code of conduct for panel members — 75

Appendix 7: Review of central list/panel members — 76

Appendix 8: Review of panel Chair — 81

Appendix 9: Panel member notes sheet — 87

Appendix 10: Quality of report — 88

Appendix 11: Checklist of additional information that may be provided by the agency — 90

Notes about the authors

Sarah Borthwick is an independent social work trainer and consultant. She provides training for foster carers, fostering social workers and panel members. She chairs a joint fostering panel for two independent fostering agencies, and an adoption panel for a local authority.

Jenifer Lord was a child placement consultant in BAAF Southern England (now CoramBAAF). She has co-run workshops for fostering panel chairs, administrators and agency advisers, and has been a member of an adoption and fostering panel. She is the principal author of *Effective Adoption Panels*, CoramBAAF's guide for adoption panel members.

Acknowledgements

Sarah Borthwick has undertaken the revision of the 2019 edition of this guide. She would like to thank the many fostering panel chairs, advisers and panel members she has worked with over the years, many of whom provided advice and information to her in undertaking this revision. She would like to give very special thanks to Elaine Dibben at CoramBAAF for her creative thinking and joint work on the new review forms. Thank you also to Janet Forbes, Kala Nobbs, Letitia Collins, Lesley Hamilton and Dylan McLees-Taylor for their helpful feedback on the new forms. She would like to give a particular thank you to Jo Francis, Shaila Shah, Leonie Jordan, Paul Adams and all the CoramBAAF staff who contributed their time and work. Finally, a special thanks to Kay Willmer for her ongoing encouragement and support.

Introduction

Fostering panels have a crucial role to play in the provision and monitoring of foster care for children. At the end of March 2018, 55,200 children in England were living in foster families, representing 73 per cent of the total number of children looked after by local authorities. Year on year, the number of children in foster care continues to increase and a diverse pool of foster carers is needed.

The Government recently emphasised that foster care is a positive option for many children and young people (*Fostering Better Outcomes*, Department for Education, 2018). In its response to two key reviews of fostering in England (House of Commons Education Committee, December 2017, and Narey and Owers, 2018), the Government set out its vision that all children and young people in foster care should benefit from high quality provision for as long as they need it (Department for Education, 2018). It identified five overarching ambitions, including:

- *Children are listened to and involved in decisions about their lives.*
- *Foster parents receive the support and respect they need and deserve to care for children.*
- *There are enough high quality fostering placements, in the right place, at the right time.*
- *Local authorities commission placements according to the needs of the child.*
- *Children experience stability regardless of permanence plan.*

Within these ambitions, the Government stated that the right foster carers should be recruited to respond to the needs of local populations. It stressed further that fostering service providers should ensure that foster carers have the skills, support and resilience to meet the needs of children in their care and that children's needs and views are the driving force of the system.

These are important aims for quality foster care, but there are difficulties experienced by many foster carers in undertaking their role (*State of the Nation's Foster Care*, Lawson and Cann, 2019). In this report, large numbers of foster carers were reported as raising concerns about the variability in support provided to them, and reinforcing the significant complexity of children and young people's needs. Foster carers need to be resilient, committed and compassionate and they need a system that fully supports them and the children whom they foster.

Making decisions about approval and terms of approval of foster carers and assessing the continuing ability of foster families to meet the complex needs of children are critical tasks. It is necessary for all agencies to have fair, sensitive and transparent processes that enable them to balance the skills and abilities of foster carers whilst keeping children's welfare paramount. Informed and well-functioning panels can assist this process.

The Fostering Services: National Minimum Standards 2011 (see Appendix 1) highlight the standards expected of panels, and the implementation of these standards should lead to the following outcome:

> *The fostering panel and decision-maker make timely, quality and appropriate recommendations/decisions in line with the overriding objective to promote the welfare of children in foster care.*
>
> (Fostering Services National Minimum Standards, 2011)

One of the reviews into fostering (Narey and Owers, 2018) queried the value and effectiveness of fostering panels and recommended a thorough assessment of their effectiveness. The Government has not, to date, commissioned such a review. Instead, in its response, it stated that it plans to work with local authorities and fostering service providers to identify what works and to tackle fostering practice issues comprehensively in innovative and flexible ways, using a network of "Fostering Trailblazers". This should lead to 'a more flexible and nuanced approach to the way that fostering panels work' (Department for Education, 2018).

How this guide will help you

This updated guide aims to set out a range of good practice approaches to the role and function of fostering panels within the required regulations and guidance. These primarily include the Fostering Services (England) Regulations 2011 (as amended) and the Children Act Guidance Volume 4: Fostering Services 2011 (as amended). Other relevant legislation is referenced. The guide brings together key messages from practice experience, reviews and standards for fostering panels. It highlights examples of creative and flexible practice in the operation of effective panels. It places particular emphasis on the need for transparency for all involved in the panel process. It highlights too that children's well-being must be at the heart of the work that panels undertake.

The guide is relevant to any panel in England that deals with fostering matters; these are in the main local authority or independent fostering provider (IFP) panels. However, this may include local authority or voluntary agency panels that consider both adoption and fostering matters. It may also include some local authority-hosted regional adoption agency (RAA) panels that consider both adoption and fostering matters as part of their remit. For example, some panels recommend dual approval of people both as prospective adopters and foster carers for children who have a high likelihood of being placed for adoption. Others may separate the agenda into adoption and fostering items over the course of a meeting. These panels must comply with the Fostering Services (England) Regulations 2011 (as amended) in the same way as any fostering panel, as well as complying with the relevant Adoption Agencies Regulations. Voluntary agencies that deal with both adoption and fostering matters must be registered as an adoption agency and a fostering agency (see *Effective Adoption Panels* (Lord and Cullen, 2016) for full information about the role and function of adoption panels).

Members of fostering panels, as well as foster carers, managers and workers in fostering services, should find this guide helpful. It is applicable to all fostering service providers, i.e. local authorities, IFPs and voluntary agencies. Although the regulations apply to England only, agencies in Wales, Scotland and Northern Ireland will also find many of the practice points applicable and useful.

What this guide covers

Chapter 1 focuses on establishing a fostering panel, including the requirements surrounding the appointment of a Chair and panel members. It also covers the expectations of the Chair and panel members and highlights the role of the administrator and agency (panel) adviser. **Chapter 2** sets out relevant legislation and agency policy and practice issues that affect panels. **Chapter 3** explores the needs of children and the potential remit of fostering panels in permanence planning. **Chapter 4** covers the key function of the panel in making recommendations regarding the suitability and approval of foster carers. It sets out the assessment process and the role and operation of the panel in making recommendations. It also explains the role of the decision-maker. **Chapter 5** focuses on family and friends (connected persons) and their particular needs when approved as foster carers for specific children. **Chapter 6** sets out the panel's role and practice in reviews of foster carers and in making recommendations regarding terminations of approval. Finally, **Chapter 7** sets out the panel's role in quality assurance and monitoring of the conduct of foster carer assessments.

A glossary of useful terms and a list of the legislation mentioned and the texts cited are provided at the end of the guide.

Appendices

The appendices contain supplementary information that agencies may find useful. They have been fully revised since the previous edition of this book. The appendices include:

- An extract from the Fostering Services: National Minimum Standards 2011

- An extract from the Training, Support and Development Standards

- Decision-making forms and qualifying determination form

- Sample job description and person specification for central list/panel members

- Sample job description and person specification for the Chair

- Sample interview questions

- Sample code of conduct for panel members

- Sample self-evaluation and review formats for central list/panel members
- Sample self-evaluation and review formats for the Chair
- Panel member notes sheet
- Quality of report forms for panel members and the panel Chair
- A checklist of additional information

Your agency may wish to use the forms provided here, or adapt them, or use their own material.

The forms in the appendices are available for agencies to copy, amend and use as they wish. All of these forms are also available as Word templates for purchase, for unlimited future use, at: www.corambaaf.org.uk/bookshop, or by contacting CoramBAAF Publications Sales at pubs.sales@corambaaf.org.uk or on 020 7520 7517. The package also includes CoramBAAF's pamphlets, *Thinking about Joining a Fostering Panel?* and *A Guide to Writing Panel Minutes*.

Notes on terminology

Throughout this guide, references to "**the Regulations**" are to the Fostering Services (England) Regulations 2011 (as amended). References to "**the Guidance**" are to the Children Act 1989 Guidance Volume 4: Fostering Services 2011 (as amended). References to any other regulations or guidance, including amending regulations, are presented using their full title.

When we refer to the **NMS**, we mean the Fostering Services: National Minimum Standards 2011.

The terms "agency" and "fostering service provider" are used interchangeably.

The 2011 NMS, regulations and guidance are available on www.education.gov.uk. They are also available in *Fostering Now*, a handy pocket guide to fostering law (Smith and Brann, 2016).

Throughout this guide, we refer to "panel members" as comprising both panel and central list members, except where context indicates otherwise.

1 Establishing a fostering panel

Membership – the regulations

The establishment of fostering panels is laid down by the Regulations. Regulation 23(1) requires the fostering service provider to:

> ...maintain a list of persons who are considered by them to be suitable to be members of a fostering panel ('the central list') including one or more social workers who have at least three years post-qualifying experience.

Regulation 23(4) requires the provider to 'constitute one or more fostering panels as necessary'. It must appoint to the panel from the persons on the central list:

(i) a person to chair the panel who, in the case of any appointment made after 1 October 2011, must be independent of the fostering service provider, and

(ii) one or two persons who may act as chair if the person appointed to chair the panel is absent or that office is vacant ('the vice chairs').

Regulation 23(5) states that 'a fostering panel may be constituted jointly by any two or more fostering service providers'. This requires that the fostering service providers have to agree which people from their respective central lists are asked to attend that panel. These providers may be local authorities or independent providers. The Regulations do not allow one fostering service to make use of the panel of another service.

Each fostering service provider must hold its own central list but there is no reason why one person should not be on two or more central lists and so, where agencies have joint panels, agencies may have identical central lists.

Regulation 23(7) requires that:

> The fostering service provider must ensure that the fostering panel has sufficient members, and that individual members have between them the experience and expertise necessary, to effectively discharge the functions of the panel.

Membership – practice issues

Panels no longer have a fixed membership or a maximum number of members. Guidance 5.4 states that:

> There is no requirement for a fostering panel to have a fixed membership, although the ability of the panel to function cohesively and with a level of consistency must be taken into account. This may best be achieved by having at least a core membership.

These core members would be invited to attend panel regularly, with other central list members attending on a less regular basis.

Guidance 5.6 states that:

> Subject to each meeting being quorate, it is for the fostering service to decide how many panel members should be present at each panel meeting. There is no limit set on the number of people who may be appointed to a panel, but a panel should not be so large as to make it difficult to chair a meeting of the panel or intimidating to prospective foster carers or anyone else attending the meeting.

Guidance 5.2 states that:

> Fostering panels are intended as multi-disciplinary bodies with a considerable element of independence from the fostering service... Panels thereby play an important quality assurance role, providing objectivity and having the ability to challenge practice ... Panels are required to give regular feedback to the fostering service.

It is therefore good practice to have a range of independent members who are able to attend.

The central list

NMS 14.1 requires that:

> The fostering service implements clear written policies and procedures on recruitment to and maintenance of the central list of persons

considered by them to be suitable to be members of a fostering panel.

NMS 14.8 requires that:

The number, skills, knowledge and experience of persons on the central list are sufficient to enable the fostering service to constitute panels that are equipped to make competent recommendations to the fostering service provider, taking into account the nature of the children and carers that the service caters for.

Guidance 5.8 recognises that panels should have available to them as required:

…people with experience of fostering, education, short break care and family and friends care, be gender balanced and reflect the diversity of the local community. People who are, or have previously been, foster carers in circumstances relevant to the matters being considered by the panel are likely to make a valuable contribution to the panel's discussion, as are their sons and daughters and people with experience of being in foster care themselves. The education and health of looked after children are also matters that are likely to feature in panel discussion and where the panel will benefit from the contribution of people with particular expertise in these areas. Elected members, as representatives of the corporate parent, may also make a valuable contribution as panel members.

Although there is no limit to the number of people on a central list, all need comprehensive checks, induction, training and reviews, as discussed elsewhere. It is likely to work best, both from the agency's and the person's point of view, if the central list is small enough to be well managed and to give everyone the opportunity to be involved with the agency and to be invited on a regular basis to attend panel.

In the case of joint panels, each agency will need to undertake the above checks and hold a personnel file for each central list member. Central list members on identical lists held by each agency will need to be aware that personnel information may be shared between agencies (but they can only share this information if the list member agrees).

Fostering service providers must comply with the General Data Protection Regulation (GDPR) and Data Protection Act (DPA) 2018 and are required to explain in writing the reasons for keeping their personal data, how long it will be kept, the circumstances in which it will be shared and security arrangements for holding and sharing their data (see Adams and Jordan, 2019, for more information).

Each agency has a responsibility for ensuring the suitability of their central list members and each agency will have its own checking policy. In practice, one agency may use the checking information obtained by the other and consider that sufficient, but they have to consider the information and not just rely on the fact that the other agency has approved them.

The Chair

Regulation 23 (4) (i) requires the fostering service provider to appoint:

…a person to chair the panel who, in the case of any appointment made after 1 October 2011, must be independent of the fostering service provider.

The regulation goes on to specify that a person is not independent of the fostering service provider if:

- they are currently approved by that provider as a foster carer;
- in the case of a local authority, they are an elected member of that authority; or
- employed by that local authority for the purpose of the fostering service or for the purposes of any of that local authority's functions relating to the protection or placement of children;
- in the case of a fostering agency, they are employed by, or are a trustee of, that fostering agency.

Guidance 5.11 states that the Chair should have:

- a sound understanding of the fostering process;
- the authority and competence to chair the panel;
- the ability to identify key issues, problems and solutions;
- excellent interpersonal, oral and written communication skills.

The Chair will need:

- the ability to chair a complex meeting where a wide variety of views may be expressed;
- the ability to lead a meeting with diplomacy and authority;
- sensitive regard to a fair and transparent process for foster carers whilst ensuring that the panel keeps children's welfare paramount;
- to be clear about the panel's recommendations and the reasons for making them;
- to encourage all members to contribute to the panel's recommendations and ensure that, where panel members have serious reservations, these are recorded in the minutes of the panel's meeting and are also attached to the panel's recommendations;
- to have responsibility for ensuring that the panel's records are accurate;
- to be clear with social workers and attending applicants that the panel only makes recommendations and should give a timescale for the agency's decision;
- to be involved in the appointment and induction of new panel members and in any consideration about terminating the appointment of a panel member;
- to have a gate-keeping role with the agency adviser to the panel, if there is one, in relation to papers coming to panel. It is advised that, where there are concerns about a report, the agency adviser and the Chair should consider whether it is adequate for submission to the panel.

Other responsibilities of the Chair are likely to be:

- involvement in the decisions on attendance of observers at panel;
- involvement when a panel member declares an interest in a case;
- involvement in deciding when an extra panel may need to be convened to consider an urgent matter;
- involvement in the preparation of an annual report on the panel's work.

The Chair may also, alongside the agency adviser, need to feed back issues of concern to the fostering service provider. There should be regular meetings between the panel Chair and the senior managers within the fostering agency. These meetings can help to monitor the work and membership of the panel and address any concerns about the panel and/or agency practice.

The Chair's role in chairing the panel meeting and facilitating the panel reaching a recommendation is described in the section entitled 'Reaching a recommendation' in Chapter 4.

Additionally, the section later in this chapter entitled, 'Review of panel members', outlines the role that the Chair, possibly with the agency adviser, will have in conducting annual reviews of panel and central list members.

The vice-chair

Regulation 23(4)(ii) requires the appointment of one or two vice-chairs who can act as Chair if the Chair is absent or no Chair is appointed. There is no requirement for the vice-chair to be independent although Guidance 5.12 says 'this would be preferable where feasible'.

Their role is clearly to deputise for the Chair when the latter is unavailable. The vice-chair therefore needs to have the ability to chair a complex meeting and have knowledge about fostering issues. It can be useful for the vice-chair to chair the panel occasionally when the Chair is present as an observer. This can allow the Chair to give feedback and to observe the dynamics of the panel meeting without having the responsibility of running the meeting. The vice-chairs could be invited to meetings with senior managers within the fostering service provider along with the Chair to discuss the progress of the fostering service and to raise any issues of concern.

Independent members

Independence is defined as for the Chair. If the Chair is unable to be present, there must be at least one independent member for the panel to be quorate. This could be the vice-chair, if independent, or another member. Guidance 5.8, quoted earlier under the heading "The central list", describes the wide range of people whose experience and expertise could be of value to a fostering panel.

A greater number of independent members can help to challenge poor practice where necessary.

Panels should be fair and be seen to be fair; greater independence can reinforce this.

It is recommended that people with experience from a variety of personal perspectives should be included on panels. This can bring a wealth of additional understanding and knowledge to the tasks required. It is very valuable to have people who are care-experienced as well as foster carers on panels. In addition, it is important to have members from black and minority ethnic groups, LGBT+[1] people and people with experience of disability so that all groups are well represented.

People who are care-experienced should be over the age of 18 years and no longer looked after.

Social work members

As previously stated, one or more social workers with at least three years' relevant post-qualifying experience must be on the fostering service provider's central list.

Regulation 23(10)(b) defines a social worker as a person who is registered as such by the Health and Care Professions Council (soon to be Social Work England) or by Social Care Wales or an equivalent in Scotland or Northern Ireland.

Guidance 5.7 confirms that the required three years' relevant post-qualifying experience 'should be in child care social work, including direct experience of fostering, either within a fostering service or in placing and supervising children in foster care'. The social worker 'would be expected to demonstrate an understanding of current legislation, policy and good practice in relation to fostering matters'. The Guidance suggests that the social worker member could advise the panel on these matters. However, there is often an agency adviser (also referred to as a panel adviser) who can do this. Provided that the social worker is not 'involved in making the decision about the foster carer's approval', they could be employed by the fostering service, but are not required to be.

Fostering service providers may on occasion find that the social work representative has to present cases too. It is therefore important to ensure that at least one of the social work representatives is able to sit on the panel at any one time. It is also possible for other social work staff to be appointed, for example, a worker specialising in working with disabled children, or a worker involved in family centre work or kinship care. It is always important to keep in mind the balance of the panel – so that at least an even mix of independent persons and agency representation is provided.

Elected member/representative of the registered provider

There is no longer a requirement to have a person in this role as a panel member. However, Guidance 5.8 states that 'elected members, as representatives of the corporate parent, may also make a valuable contribution as panel members'.

Recruitment

Recruiting members to the central list should involve an open process, encouraging applications from a wide range of people. Many members have been recruited through personal recommendations about individuals and although this can work well, it can also lead to members being drawn from a rather narrow group of people already known to the agency.

It can be helpful to advertise locally or through user groups; these may be useful ways of finding independent members with personal experience of fostering. An internal newsletter could be advertised widely throughout the fostering agency to encourage a range of applications from social work staff. In all cases it is good practice to provide a job description and person specification for the member. Applicants can then be shortlisted and interviewed against open and clear criteria. (See Appendix 5)

Sample job descriptions and person specifications for central list/panel members and Chairs are also included in the appendices.

Agency adviser to the panel

This post is not required for a fostering panel although it is for an adoption panel. As mentioned in the social work member section, the Guidance suggests that this panel member could give advice within panel. However, as listed here, there are many other tasks both before and after panel that need doing and it can be helpful if that person also

---

1 The term "LGBT+" is commonly used to mean "lesbian, gay, bisexual and transgender, and related communities".

attends panel in an advisory capacity. The agency adviser is not a voting member and should not participate in making recommendations. The agency adviser to the fostering panel has the following role:

- co-ordinating and agreeing the agenda;
- ensuring that paperwork has been quality assured by managers;
- ensuring that paperwork for panel members is sent out in good time either electronically or through the post;
- advising the panel on regulations, guidance, policy and procedures;
- providing updates on matters presented;
- taking feedback from and to the panel and the fostering service about practice issues;
- being involved in the recruitment and appointment of panel members;
- arranging induction and training of panel members.

Good practice would suggest that the agency adviser to fostering panels should be involved in overseeing the quality of reports provided to panel. The agency adviser should liaise with appropriate staff to ensure that the reports provided are of good quality. Where there are concerns about a report, the adviser and the Chair should consider whether it is adequate for submission or whether the papers should be withdrawn.

It is very important that the agency adviser has the authority to advise the panel and to be in a position to take back difficult issues to and from the agency. The adviser therefore needs to be in an influential position within the agency and both confident and able to give objective advice. The relevant service manager or a team manager with responsibility for the fostering team may have been given this role. However, this can mean that the adviser is the line manager of staff presenting reports and on occasion there can be a conflict of interest between the role of line manager and that of agency adviser. Strategies for dealing with such conflicts need to be in place, including having regular meetings with the Chair. Many agencies have therefore appointed another manager to this role to avoid conflicts of interest.

As now required for adoption panel members, the agency adviser, along with the Chair, could be involved in conducting annual reviews of central list/panel members. This is described in the section later in this chapter, "Review of panel members".

Medical advice and legal advice

NMS 14.6 requires that 'fostering panels have access to medical expertise and legal advice, as required'. Guidance 5.24 states that:

> *This is best provided by the identification of a named medical adviser and legal adviser to the panel, who might also be shared with an adoption panel or another fostering panel.*

Such advisers are not required to be members of the fostering panel (although they may be) and may supply information either in writing or by attending panel meetings as required.

Although there is no requirement, it would be good practice to appoint an agency medical adviser or other health professional as a core member or adviser to the panel, if possible. The medical adviser has a key role in advising on adult health issues as well as issues relating to children in foster care. If it is not possible for the medical adviser to be appointed to the panel, it has been found to be very helpful if they can see the applicants' assessment report (and the assessment report about the child, if applicable) as well as the medical forms in order to provide written advice.

If the agency medical adviser does not attend the panel, it can be helpful for the agency to arrange six-monthly meetings between the Chair, the agency adviser, other relevant managers and the decision-maker to pick up on any health practice matters that may have arisen.

Checks on panel members

These apply to everyone on the agency's central list. They are listed in NMS 19.3 and include:

- identity checks;
- criminal records check from the Disclosure and Barring Service (DBS);
- checks to confirm qualifications that are a requirement and those that are considered by the fostering service to be relevant;

- at least two references, preferably one from a current employer;
- checks to confirm the right to work in the UK;
- further checks if a person has lived out of the UK.

Everyone must be interviewed as part of the selection process and have references checked. Telephone enquiries must be made to each referee to verify the written references.

Although not a requirement, repeat DBS checks on central list members are undertaken by many agencies every three years.

Tenure

There is no requirement in the Regulations about tenure. Guidance 5.13 states that:

> There is no prescribed maximum or minimum tenure, although the fostering services should plan and manage turnover in such a way that it avoids the need to replace a large proportion of members in any one year. This may best be achieved through establishing clarity of role and reviewing appointments to panel and those who are included on the central list regularly. Equally the fostering service will need to be mindful of the need to have a certain level of turnover to provide for a fresh perspective.

There is nothing to stop an agency from appointing people to its central list for a set period if it wishes, which would be reviewed and could be extended if appropriate.

Resignation

Regulation 23(8) specifies that:

> Any panel member may resign at any time by giving one month's notice in writing to the fostering service provider which appointed them.

This applies to anyone on the central list.

Termination of appointment

There is also provision for the fostering service provider to terminate the appointment of members. Regulation 23(9) states that:

> Where a fostering service provider is of the opinion that any member of the fostering panel is unsuitable or unable to continue as a panel member, it may terminate that member's appointment at any time by giving him notice in writing.

Guidance 5.17 clarifies that the notice given does not have to be one month. This applies to anyone on the central list.

An exit interview following a resignation or termination of appointment could be helpfully offered.

Panel membership agreement

Guidance 5.14 states that:

> Before appointing any panel member or including them on the central list, the fostering service should inform them in writing of their performance objectives, which should include participation in induction and training and safeguarding the confidentiality of records and information submitted to the panel. Panel members should sign an acceptance form to record their agreement to these objectives.

NMS 23 requires that:

- Persons joining the central list of persons considered suitable to be fostering panel members are provided with an opportunity to observe a fostering panel meeting.
- Each person on the central list is given induction training which is completed within 10 weeks of joining the central list.
- Each person on the central list is given the opportunity of attending an annual joint training day with the fostering services fostering staff.
- Each person on the central list has access to appropriate training and skills development and is kept abreast of relevant changes to legislation and guidance.

A comprehensive written agreement would include:

- attendance at an agreed number of panel meetings, if specified;
- participation in induction and training;

- safeguarding the confidentiality of records and information submitted to the panel, signing a confidentiality statement;
- commitment to a code of conduct for panel members, setting out the agency's performance objectives (see Appendix 6).

The fostering service provider, for its part, should make a commitment to:

- provide induction training and written information to help prepare the central list members for the task, the written information to be updated as required;
- arrange at least an annual training day for all central list members;
- offer individual support and help, as far as practicable, should the member need or request this;
- send all the necessary information for each case, either electronically or by post, to be received five working days in advance of the date when the case will be considered (NMS 14.3);
- assist members, if necessary, in the provision of a suitable, secure storage space for confidential panel papers while they are in the panel member's home;
- provision of the use of a laptop or tablet, should papers be sent electronically;
- reimburse travel costs and consider the payment of a fee for reading panel papers and panel attendance;
- make available an opportunity for members to make representations or complaints to the agency;
- discuss any concerns about a panel member's behaviour or conduct, possibly with reference to the code of conduct for panel members (see Appendix 6). If these concerns cannot be resolved, the agency will put in writing the reasons why it is ending the member's appointment to the central list.

Review of panel members

Guidance 5.15 states that:

Each panel member's performance, including that of the Chair, should be reviewed annually, against agreed performance objectives. The service's decision-maker should review the performance of the panel Chair, and for this purpose may attend a proportion of panel meetings, but only as an observer. Views about the Chair's performance should be sought from other panel members and from those who attend panel meetings, such as prospective foster carers and social workers who present reports to panel. For all other panel members, the panel Chair should conduct the performance review.

All central list members are potential panel members and should have an annual review. If the person has not sat on a panel during the year, it will be difficult to do a review and it might be decided that they should not remain on the central list.

Fully revised forms for conducting the review are included in the appendices.

The review could provide a useful opportunity for the member to talk about any issues that may have inhibited their performance. These may include, for instance, a panel process that allows forceful or voluble panel members always to get in first with issues and questions or an agenda that is so tight that there is inadequate time for all panel members to contribute. It may also include discussion on the rationale for appointing people from the central list to sit on a panel and why this member has or has not been called upon. It will also provide an opportunity for constructive feedback by the panel Chair and agency adviser on the panel member's contribution to panel meetings. It is good practice for this to be evidenced by feedback from the other panel members and from presenting social workers and applicants who have attended panel. The need for further input or training should be agreed and arrangements made to provide this.

Brief feedback sheets, for presenting social workers and prospective carers who attend panel, on the process as a whole, the role of the Chair and the contribution of any individual panel members should be completed. It is also useful to ask panel members to provide written comments on the panel as a whole, on the Chair's contribution and on any other particular dynamics or issues (see Appendix 7 for sample forms).

Group performance reviews

Some agencies arrange for panel member reviews to be undertaken by the Chair as a whole group exercise. Flip chart papers with headings are provided for each member and all members present are provided with sticky notes. Headings may include:

- What do you feel X brings to the panel that you feel is particularly helpful?
- If they were to change something, what could X do to help you and others at the panel?
- What support would benefit you or other panel members?
- What training would be helpful for you or other panel members?
- What do you feel you bring to the panel?
- What do you think you or the panel might do differently/better?

Each member is asked to note answers in relation to the first two questions on their sticky notes, relating to all panel members. These are displayed on the flip charts to prompt discussion and changes to practice if necessary. Practice experience has found that this can be a good team building tool and as effective at bringing out issues as having a one-to-one appraisal.

Fees for panel members

Regulation 23(6) states that:

A local authority may pay to any member of a fostering panel constituted by them such fee as they determine, being a fee of a reasonable amount.

Guidance 5.18 adds that expenses may also be paid and that fees 'may take account of preparation time'. It further states that 'payment of a reasonable fee to the Chair or any other member of a fostering panel does not, in itself, compromise independence'. It confirms that fees may be paid by any fostering service.

Payment of fees allows a wider recruitment of panel members. It allows more people to attend, not just those who can afford to give their time on a voluntary basis or those people whose employers are prepared to donate their time. The Chair has a wider range of responsibilities than other panel members and will usually be paid a higher fee. A higher fee for the vice-chair could be considered when he or she is required to chair.

Quorum

Regulation 24(1) requires that 'no business may be conducted by a fostering panel unless at least the following meet as the panel'. These are:

- the Chair or a vice-chair;
- a social worker with at least three years' relevant post-qualifying experience;
- at least three other members, or four if it is a joint panel with other fostering service providers;
- if the Chair is not present, there must be at least one independent member present, either the vice-chair or a member, who could be the social work member if they are independent of the agency.

Declaring an interest

There can be situations where a panel member knows or has worked with the applicant or approved foster carer to be considered by the panel. It is important that the panel member should declare an interest in such situations. The panel member should say whether they think this knowledge will prejudice their consideration of the case. If they think so, they should not participate in that case and it is best if they leave the room. If the panel member does not think their knowledge will affect their consideration of the case, it will be the responsibility of the Chair, possibly with the help of the agency adviser, to make the final decision. It is important for panel members to alert the agency adviser or panel Chair as early as possible to avoid a possible problem over quoracy.

Non-panel members

Social workers presenting cases to the fostering panel will need to attend the panel to do this.

Sometimes, if the worker is new to the agency or presenting contentious cases, it will be important that their manager also attends.

NMS 14.5 allows foster carers and prospective foster carers who attend a panel meeting at which their approval is being discussed 'to bring a supporter to the panel if they wish'. Central list members are required by NMS 23.8 to 'be provided with an opportunity to observe a fostering panel meeting'. Occasionally other social workers and allied professionals may attend to observe the panel.

Good practice suggests that a maximum of two observers should attend at any one time and the Chair should be consulted. Observers should sign a confidentiality bond and the agreement of foster carers whose cases are being heard by the panel should be sought. Further, there may be occasions where the issues being considered are so sensitive that observers should not attend (e.g. where a termination of approval is being considered in a case of serious child protection concerns in respect of the foster carer).

Sending information to panel members

Some agencies continue to send reports on cases to be considered by panel in paper form through the post. However, more and more agencies are doing this electronically. This may be done by emailing pdf documents that can be downloaded from secure portals, or putting them on a "web shelf" like Sharepoint or Charms, and providing tablets onto which reports are downloaded. *Paperless Fostering and Adoption Panels* (BAAF, 2014) provides useful advice on the issues associated with providing electronic information.

Panel information leaflet and member profiles

Many agencies provide an information leaflet outlining the role and function of the fostering panel, along with profiles of people on the central list. Both of these should be made available to applicants and approved carers prior to attending the panel.

Administration

Good administrative arrangements are essential for the effective functioning of a panel. An appropriate manager should be responsible for panel support. They should ensure that sufficient administrative support is provided for the efficient performance of the tasks listed below. Any necessary training should be provided for the staff concerned.

The fostering service provider should, in conjunction with the Chair and panel members, determine the number and usual length of meetings, the number of cases to be considered at each, and whether or not the forms need anonymising. The format of panel minutes should be agreed, including the amount of detail to be recorded and whether members' contributions to the panel's deliberations should be attributed by name. The administrator should be provided with necessary training to undertake the tasks detailed below.

Main administrative functions

Before panel meetings:

- Production of an annual schedule of meetings.
- Maintenance of a panel booking system, including a process for urgent cases.
- Notification to social workers of panel schedule and deadlines.
- Arrangement of accommodation and refreshments for meetings with, if practicable, a private waiting area for applicants and others attending the meeting.
- Maintenance of records of central list members, their tenure, confidentiality bonds, etc.
- Preparation of agendas.
- Working with the agency adviser, liaison with social workers and managers as required to ensure that the panel's requirements are met. This should include ensuring that social workers submit reports in good time, in the quantity required and in conformity with the panel's requirements.
- Responding to enquiries from social workers and foster carers about appearances before the panel, panel procedures and reporting requirements.
- Receiving of reports submitted and bringing to the attention of the agency adviser any apparent gaps.
- NMS 14.3 requires that 'all necessary information is provided to panel members at least five working days in advance of the panel meeting to enable full and proper consideration'. Papers must be sent out in as secure a way as possible, either electronically or through the post.
- Ensuring that appropriate central list members are able to attend meetings to ensure a quorum.
- Liaison with the Chair about requests from observers.
- Ensuring that meeting and waiting rooms have disability access, are prepared for the meeting, that name plates/badges are ready, that spare reports are

available, that refreshments are ready, that recording equipment if used is functioning, etc. A hearing loop and/or interpreters should be available if required.

- Ensuring that telephone or video conferencing facilities such as Skype are available when needed.

At the meeting:

- Taking minutes, noting, in particular, recommendations made and reasons given (see below).

- Drawing to the attention of the Chair any matters requiring their attention.

- Collection of papers at the end of the meeting.

After the meeting:

- Drafting minutes, including recommendations made and reasons given.

- Submitting draft minutes to the Chair and panel members for checking.

- Ensuring that the decision-maker receives the minutes and any other papers required for the decision to be made.

- Ensuring that applicants, foster carers and social workers are notified in writing of decisions.

- Providing the social worker with a copy of relevant minutes.

- Maintaining full records of panel business, including agenda, reports and minutes.

- Maintaining statistical records for performance monitoring, government returns and the annual report.

Minutes

Regulation 24(2) requires that 'a fostering panel shall make a written record of its proceedings and the reasons for its recommendations'.

Good minuting of panel meetings is essential and should be done by someone who is not a panel member. The minutes should cover the key issues and views expressed by panel members, rather than be a verbatim record of the meeting. If it is not possible to reach a consensus on a recommendation, the panel minutes should set out clearly the view of any dissenting panel member. The pamphlet, *A Guide to Writing Panel Minutes* (Pratt, 2019), may be useful. (It is included in the package of Word forms that can be purchased separately from this book, as detailed on page 3).

The Chair is responsible for ensuring that 'written minutes of panel meetings are accurate and clearly cover the key issues and views expressed by panel members and record the reasons for its recommendations' (NMS 14.7). NMS 14.9 requires that the decision-maker makes a decision 'within seven working days of receipt of the recommendation and final set of panel minutes'. All panel members must be offered the opportunity to check the draft minutes before they are sent to the decision-maker. In practice, many agencies send the draft minutes securely and electronically to panel members who are asked to send back any suggested amendments. These are considered and amended accordingly by the Chair who is responsible for the final set of minutes. Because timing is tight, panel members and the Chair are usually given a very short timescale to complete their checks.

Sharing panel minutes

The fostering agency has discretion to share relevant parts of the panel minutes and may decide this is appropriate to inform a fostering decision. Some agencies share panel minutes with applicants to foster and foster carers who have been reviewed by the panel. The foster carer may have been at the panel meeting, and the record of the discussion leading to the panel's recommendation to the decision-maker is likely to be the basis of the reasons for the final decision and generally will not contain third party information. Sharing of minutes should be done securely and any restrictions on further sharing should be explicit and consistent with the agency's data protection policies and procedures.

Applicants to foster and foster carers can ask to see the personal data about them in the minutes under the Data Protection Act 2018. However, a foster carer or applicant is not entitled to see references unless the referee gives permission for their reference to be shared. The agency has discretion about whether to share information in the minutes and decisions about this should be guided by data protection principles of transparency and accuracy. Data about another person, for example, a person who may have provided information in a reference, should not be shared without that person's consent. The fostering service provider may, if there is a sound factual basis for such a decision, withhold personal data information if it considers that sharing would be likely to adversely affect its ability to meet its social work responsibilities '...by reason of the fact that serious harm to the physical or mental health or condition of the data subject or any other person would be likely to be caused'. The agency should consult with its data protection adviser if there are concerns about what information to share, and a record must be made of the reasons for any decision about sharing or withholding personal data.

The court has the power to require disclosure of minutes if information recorded is relevant to the proceedings. If the agency considers that it is not in the interests of a person identified in the minutes for their personal data to be shared with all the parties to the proceedings, the agency will need to persuade the court about whether and what redactions should be made. In care proceedings, the Children's Guardian may also have a view about this. The Children's Guardian can only have access to the child's record, not the foster carers' case record. If the local authority has a permanence panel that considers matching for long-term fostering or a connected person's fostering placement, the matching panel minutes will be on the child's case records and the Children's Guardian is entitled to see these and may request that the minutes be shared with the court.

Fostering inspection

There is a single inspection framework to focus on the effectiveness of local authority services and arrangements to help and protect children, the experience of children looked after, including adoption, fostering, the use of residential care, and children who return home. This is now on a three-year cycle. There is a separate framework for the inspection of IFPs.

Central list members will be invited to complete an Ofsted questionnaire regarding the services provided. An inspector will wish to see the last three sets of panel minutes, they may observe a panel meeting, and will usually interview the Chair. The inspector will also look at central list members' files.

Remit of the panel

The fostering panel has several very important functions, which are listed in Regulation 25.

These are:

- to make recommendations about the approval of foster carers;
- to recommend any terms of approval;
- to consider the first review of carers, and any other review if requested by the fostering service provider, and to recommend the continuing approval of carers;
- to advise, where appropriate, on the procedure for reviews of carers and periodically to monitor their effectiveness;
- to oversee the conduct of assessments carried out by the fostering service provider;
- to give advice, and make recommendations, on other matters or cases referred to it by the fostering service provider, including terminations of approval in some cases.

These functions are fully discussed in later chapters.

2 Agency policy and practice issues

Relevant legislation and guidance

Children Act 1989 and the Care Planning, Placement and Case Review (England) Regulations 2010

The Act requires that, when placing a looked after child in foster care, the local authority should, if reasonably practicable and consistent with the welfare of the child, ensure that they are placed near home, without disruption to education, and that siblings are accommodated together. The local authority should also, if reasonably practicable and consistent with the child's welfare, arrange for the child to live with a relative or friend (a "connected person").

These regulations provide the regulatory framework for care planning, placements and case reviews. Part 3 deals with placements, including the matters to be taken into account when assessing a foster carer's suitability to care for a child, emergency placements and temporary approvals.

Fostering Services (England) Regulations 2011 (referred to as "the Regulations" in this guide)

These provide the regulatory framework for the management and conduct of the fostering service, the approval of foster carers, the making of placements and the establishment and functioning of fostering panels. These regulations are referred to throughout the guide and are the key set of regulations in relation to fostering panels.

Both sets of regulations above have been extensively amended. Key sets of amending regulations in relation to fostering panels are set out below.

Care Planning, Placement and Case Review and Fostering Services (Miscellaneous Amendments) Regulations 2013

These make amendments to the Care Planning, Placement and Case Review Regulations 2010 and the Regulations. They include the introduction of a regulatory framework for the temporary approval of a prospective adopter as a foster carer for a named child. Additionally, they set out the regulatory framework for delegating authority for decision making to foster carers. They also set out some changes to assessments of foster carers where they are approved by another fostering provider and are moving agency. They introduce a Stage 1 and Stage 2 process for foster carer assessments. They also enable changes in a foster carer's terms of approval to be agreed by a fostering service provider and a foster carer without delay.

Adoption and Care Planning (Miscellaneous Amendments) Regulations 2014

These make amendments to the Care Planning, Placement and Case Review Regulations 2010. They cover the placement of children under section 22C(9B)(c) of the Children Act 1989 with foster carers who are also approved prospective adopters.

Care Planning and Fostering (Miscellaneous Amendments) (England) Regulations 2015

These amend various sections of the Care Planning, Placement and Case Review Regulations 2010, the Regulations and the Independent Review of Determinations (Adoption and Fostering) Regulations 2009. For the first time, they introduce a definition of a long-term fostering placement and set out the conditions that must be complied with before a child can be placed in a long-term fostering placement. They also make provision for the frequency of review meetings and social work visits in such placements. They also set out arrangements that a local authority must make when they are considering ceasing to look after a child. They make clear that where a 'brief report' is presented to panel during Stage 2 of a foster carer assessment, the fostering panel must either request the fostering service to complete the assessment and prepare a full report, or recommend that the person is not suitable to foster.

Children Act 1989 Guidance and Regulations, Volume 2: Care Planning, Placement and Case Review, June 2015

This updates and consolidates the Children Act 1989 Guidance and Regulations, Volume 2: Care Planning, Placement and Case Review, previously published in 2010. It expands on the above regulations. References in this guide are to the consolidated version, which incorporates various amendments, including:

- Delegation of authority, July 2013;
- Early permanence placements and approval of prospective adopters as foster carers, July 2014;
- Permanence, long-term foster placements and ceasing to look after a child, March 2015.

Children Act 1989 Guidance and Regulations, Volume 4, Fostering Services, 2011

This guidance relates to and expands on the requirements of the Regulations.

This volume of guidance has also been amended, but it has not been consolidated.

Amendments relevant to fostering panels include the removal of paragraphs 3.9–3.24 dealing with delegation of authority. Replacement guidance was provided by the July 2013 amendments to Volume 2. This replacement guidance can now be found in paragraphs 3.192–3.223 of the consolidated Volume 2.

Other amendments include the process for assessing and approving foster carers (see below).

Assessment and Approval of Foster Carers: Amendments to the Children Act 1989 Guidance and Regulations, Volume 4: Fostering Services, July 2013

This covers the Stage 1 and Stage 2 assessment and approval process of foster carers. It also provides guidance on foster carers' reviews and terminations of approvals including changes to terms of approval. It clarifies that all decisions following a review of a foster carer's approval should be made by the decision-maker.

Family and Friends Care: Statutory Guidance for Local Authorities 2011

This covers situations where a child is placed with someone already known to or related to them.

National Minimum Standards (NMS) for Fostering Services 2011

These cover in more detail the operation of fostering services, including the panel. They are the Standards against which the service is inspected.

Other relevant legislation and guidance

Fostering for Adoption: Practice Guidance 2017

The Good Practice Guide, *The Role of Fostering for Adoption in Achieving Early Permanence for Children* (Dibben and Howorth, 2017, available online at https://bit.ly/2L2oHga or to purchase from CoramBAAF), sets out the most recent guidance regarding the assessment and approval of prospective adopters under Fostering for Adoption.

"Staying Put" Arrangements for Care Leavers aged 18 and above to stay on with their former foster carers DfE, DWP and HMRC Guidance, May 2013

This guidance sets out the different "Staying Put" arrangements whereby young people aged 18 years or older who were previously looked after remain living with their former foster carer (who may also remain a foster carer for younger children).

Children and Families Act 2014

Section 12 amends the Children Act 1989. This introduces child arrangements orders (replacing residence and contact orders) for children affected by private proceedings. It also introduces time limits for care proceedings.

Children and Social Work Act 2017

Amongst other matters, the Act aims to improve support for looked after children and care leavers. It includes a requirement on local authorities to publish information about the services they offer to care leavers. Local authorities have a duty to appoint a personal adviser for care leavers until the age of 25 and to make advice and information available to promote the educational achievement of looked after children. A national Child Safeguarding Practice Review Panel has been established and operational since June 2018 and a new regulator, Social Work England, which will be the registration body for social workers, is introduced.

General policies and practice relating to fostering

Statement of purpose

The Regulations, NMS and Guidance 4.1–4.2 require every fostering service provider to produce a written statement of its aims and objectives and of the services and facilities it provides. A copy of this could be given to central list members.

Children's guide

The Regulations, NMS and Guidance 4.1–4.4 also require the agency to provide a children's guide, summarising its statement of purpose and giving information about its complaints procedure. Members could ask to see a copy of this. CoramBAAF's children's guide, *Fostering: What it is and what it means*, by Shaila Shah, is ideal for this purpose.

Agency policies

All agencies will have a range of child care, safeguarding and child protection policies and procedures. Members need to be aware of these and could ask to see copies.

Foster carer handbook

NMS 21.10 and Guidance 5.69 require that fostering service providers give their foster carers a handbook or electronic equivalent that covers policies, procedures, guidance, legal information and insurance details. This is updated regularly.

Fostering panel policies and procedures

NMS 14 requires that:

- *The fostering service implements clear written policies and procedures on recruitment to and maintenance of the central list of persons considered by them to be suitable to be members of a fostering panel (the central list) and on constitution of fostering panels (NMS 14.1).*

- *…panels provide a quality assurance feedback to the fostering service provider on the quality of reports being presented to panel (NMS 14.2).*

- *All necessary information is provided to panel members at least five working days in advance of the panel meeting… (NMS 14.3).*

- *The fostering panel makes its recommendation on the suitability of a prospective foster carer within eight months of receipt of the prospective foster carer's application to be assessed (NMS 14.4).*

- *Foster carers and prospective foster carers are given the opportunity to attend and be heard at all panel meetings at which their approval is being discussed and to bring a supporter to the panel if they wish (NMS 14.5).*

Guidance 5.22 adds to this.

Agencies may have higher expectations than the National Minimum Standards. For example, some agencies require that decisions should be made on the approval of prospective foster carers within six months rather than eight months.

Checks and references

Panel members should be aware of the range of checks and references that the agency requires of a prospective foster carer as these may be more than the statutory minimum. *Undertaking Checks and References in Fostering and Adoption Assessments* (Adams, 2017) provides detailed advice and information. There is further discussion about this later in this chapter and in Chapter 4.

Specific issues that panel members will need to consider

The agency may have a formal policy or a clear view on some of the issues identified in this section. Central list members should be made aware of agency policies before being appointed and should be broadly in agreement with them. However, panel members have a responsibility to consider each individual case carefully on its own merits.

There is no such thing as the "perfect" family or the "ideal" match. There will be an element of risk in any recommendation made. It is important that strengths, limitations and support needs are identified and ways to address any limitations are clearly specified. However, panel members should also be clear that the child's welfare is their paramount consideration and that it will sometimes be necessary to reach a view that a foster carer applicant is not suitable to foster, or an approved foster carer is no longer suitable to foster.

NMS 13 and amended Guidance 5.26–5.38 cover the recruitment, assessment and approval of foster carers.

Couples and partnerships

Many people who come forward for assessment as foster carers are in a couple relationship: married, in a civil partnership, or otherwise in a committed intimate relationship. Some may be in a partnership, such as a mother and daughter in the same household who wish to foster together. Most couples or partnerships will be assessed jointly as they will be "sharing the care" of children in their household (see Guidance 5.31). However, some individuals may have a partner who does not wish to be involved in fostering and their involvement with a child will need careful consideration. The main issue to explore is whether the individuals would be "sharing the care" of a child. Practice Note 65, *Decisions about the Assessments of Couples and Other Partnerships in Foster Care (England)* (CoramBAAF, 2017) offers helpful advice on this.

Single carers

There are many people approved as foster carers who are single. They may be able to provide considerable one-to-one time to fostered children and undertake the fostering task very successfully. Some children may relate better to a lone female or male carer if they have negative associations from the past regarding parenting figures. Issues of emotional and practical support, work arrangements and health factors, however, need to be considered. Should a single carer start a new adult partnership, this will need to be assessed. Guidance 5.31 requires that:

> Where a single foster carer takes a partner who will be sharing the care of any foster children,
> they must discuss this with their supervising social worker so that agreement can be reached about the best way to update their assessment and to assess the partner for approval as a foster carer within an appropriate timescale.

Lesbian and gay carers

There is a useful Good Practice Guide, *Recruiting, Assessing and Supporting Lesbian and Gay Adopters* (de Jong and Donnelly, 2015), much of which is of relevance to fostering.

Lesbians and gay men have been fostering or adopting children successfully for many years and a positive and inclusive message should be given to all foster carer applicants by agencies. Nevertheless, particular attention may still be needed to consider any support needs required as the family may experience discrimination or prejudice. De Jong and Donnelly (2015) note that the issue of male and female role models often continues to be raised within assessments and at panels. They comment that it is important to consider that 'same-sex couples and single applicants don't usually live in a "single sex bubble"'. They note that 'what is important is the strength and diversity of the applicants' social network, which should of course be part of any assessment, regardless of the applicants' sexuality or relationship status'. It is therefore the skills, qualities and experience of people to meet the needs of children in foster care that is the focus of consideration. Cocker and Brown (2010) suggest a useful model to include in assessments of all applicants, whether heterosexual, lesbian or gay. The model covers sexual orientation, previous sexual relationship histories, current relationships, the expression of intimacy, integration into the community, the "not so nice bits", i.e. dealing with stress and thinking about patterns and gaps within the stories being told. It is helpful for panel members to have opportunities to explore their own values and attitudes, and training should be provided.

Transgender carers

There is increasing recognition that people who are transgender have been overlooked with regard to their potential as foster carers and adopters (see Practice Note 69, *Assessing and Supporting Transgender Foster Carers and Adopters*,

CoramBAAF, 2018b). As stated in the Practice Note, there is no reason to think that transgender applicants are any less likely to be good foster carers than non-transgender people:

> *Research and practice knowledge tells us…the most important attributes of carers are nothing to do with gender and sexuality.*
>
> (Brown, 2017)

It is important that social workers and panel members have regard to the many good practice points, as set out in the Practice Note. This includes having an inclusive and anti-oppressive approach to the work. As for any applicant, the key component of the assessment is the individual's parenting capacity. How identity matters interface with being a foster carer should also be considered. As for any other minority groups, exploration of the capacity to deal with bullying and oppression should be undertaken alongside identification of any particular support needs. Training for social workers and panel members should be provided in gender variance and expression. Knowledge can be lacking and there is prejudice and anxiety. The Chair and panel members need to be both non-discriminatory and confident in handling an assessment and coming to a fair and evidenced recommendation. Has your agency developed policies and practice regarding transgender carers and does it provide training?

Divorce or previously failed partnerships

Panel members need to assess whether this is a pattern that could be repeated. If the carer has parented jointly with a previous partner, significant efforts should be made to interview this partner and appropriate weight attached to their views.

Health and disability issues

Medical conditions or disabilities should not necessarily rule out applicants. A health risk assessment should be made by the medical adviser and their advice will be extremely important. However, panel members should weigh up the advice alongside other qualities that the prospective carers possess before reaching a recommendation. *Undertaking a Health Assessment* (Merredew and Sampeys, 2017) provides useful advice and information.

The following health-related lifestyle factors should also be considered.

Mental health

It is estimated that one in four people in the UK will experience some form of mental ill health during their lifetime. As with other illnesses, a full history and analysis should be undertaken in the assessment. Using prescribed medication should be explored but it should be noted that someone who is stable and functioning well on medication can be a successful foster carer. The ability to manage stress and seek and receive support will be a key consideration (see Adams, 2017).

Smoking

There is very clear evidence that smoking causes health problems for the smoker but also that passive smoking can damage the health of others. Practice Note 68 (CoramBAAF, 2018a) outlines the very significant harm to children who live in an environment where there is daily exposure to tobacco smoke, at home and/or in the car. There is also research evidence that children living with adults who smoke are three times more likely to become smokers themselves (World Health Organisation, 1999). Practice Note 68 recommends that children under five or those with disabilities or respiratory problems should not be placed with carers who smoke. It also recommends that all substitute carers should be proactively encouraged to stop smoking and further recommends that new applicants should not be allowed to foster young children until they have given up smoking for a minimum of 12 months. Does your agency have a policy in relation to applicants who smoke?

Some children are placed with family and friends carers who smoke. The benefits of being placed with the family and friends carers will have been carefully weighed and considered. Nevertheless, the health risks should be outlined and the family and friends carers encouraged to quit smoking and implement a smoke-free home and car.

In recent years, electronic cigarettes have become more popular. Gould (2015) notes in *Promoting the Health of Children in Public Care*, edited by Merredew and Sampeys, that e-cigarettes appear to have some positive benefits for smokers wishing to quit and the risk to children from passive smoke is lower. However, she also notes that there may be risks in terms of unhelpful role modelling and a possible "re-normalising" of smoking. Liquid nicotine is also highly toxic. NICE Guideline 92 (2018) states that:

> The evidence suggests that e-cigarettes are substantially less harmful to health than smoking but are not risk-free. The evidence in this area is still developing, including the evidence of long-term health impact.

Does your agency have a policy relating to e-cigarettes?

Weight issues

Obesity can cause health problems, as can anorexia or other eating disorders. Is there evidence of limited mobility or of unhealthy eating patterns, either of which could affect parenting capacity? Advice from the medical adviser will be important. *Evaluating Obesity in Substitute Carers* (Mather and Lehner, 2010) provides very useful information and advice for health professionals, social workers and panel members. The role of the medical adviser is reinforced further by Gould (2015) in *Promoting the Health of Children in Public Care*. It is important to note that the recommendation about whether to approve an obese applicant is a joint one in which the medical adviser, social workers and panel members all have an important role.

Alcohol consumption

Excessive alcohol consumption can cause health problems. Alcohol may also be associated with violence and physical abuse for many looked after children. In January 2016, new guidelines for alcohol consumption were issued by the Department of Health stating that both men and women should not regularly drink more than 14 units of alcohol per week. They should also have several drink-free days per week. Does your agency have a policy on this?

The Drinkaware website (www.drinkaware.co.uk) includes useful information on the impact of alcohol on health and well-being. An applicant's understanding of how children may have experienced parental alcohol misuse should be included in the social worker's assessment (see Gould, 2015).

Age

There is no minimum age for fostering. Exceptionally, a young person, who would usually be at least 18, could be considered as a foster carer perhaps for a younger sibling. However, most foster carers will need the maturity to work with parents as well as with children and young people, and will usually be at least 21, if not older.

Experienced foster carers often continue fostering into their 60s and 70s. However, many agencies do have a usual retirement age for their carers and panel members should be aware of this. Agencies may recruit new carers in their late 50s or possibly older.

In every case, with both younger than average and older than average prospective carers, panel members will need to consider the particular skills and experience of the individual and the particular fostering task for which they are being considered, before making a recommendation.

Child's position in the family and age gaps between children

The wishes and feelings of existing children in the family must be fully explored and covered in the reports to panel. It can be helpful to have a written or drawn contribution from existing children. What is the child's understanding of fostering, and how prepared are they? How will they feel about no longer being the oldest or the youngest child in the family while a foster child is placed? Research (Sellick *et al*, 2004) indicates that permanent placements are at higher risk of not working out if a child is placed close in age to an existing child in the family.

"Children who foster" play a vital role in the fostering service which their parents provide. Studies have indicated their particular support needs. Does your agency offer any support groups or other forms of support to the children of foster carers? The book *We are Fostering*, written by Jean Camis, and a board game titled *Welcome to our Family* (both available from CoramBAAF), are two useful resources for work with families who are going to foster.

Discipline issues

Schedule 5.2 (c) of the Regulations prohibits the use of corporal punishment by foster carers. Panel members need to ensure that this has been made clear to carers and that they are in agreement. Have they smacked their own children? What alternatives for managing challenging behaviours do they or would they use? What is their understanding of attachment and the effects of trauma on children and their behaviour? What ongoing training and support will the agency offer on managing challenging behaviour?

Accommodation

NMS 10.6 requires that:

> *In the foster home, each child over the age of three should have their own bedroom. If this is not possible, the sharing of a bedroom is agreed by each child's responsible authority and each child has their own area within the bedroom. Before seeking agreement for the sharing of a bedroom, the fostering service provider takes into account any potential for bullying, any history of abuse or abusive behaviour, the wishes of the children concerned and all other pertinent facts. The decision-making process and outcome of the assessment are recorded in writing where bedroom sharing is agreed.*

Health and safety issues

A health and safety checklist covering the foster home and garden will have been completed and may be included with the paperwork for panel. Carers must be provided with written guidelines on their health and safety responsibilities (NMS 10.2, 10.3, 10.4). Has this been done?

The Good Practice Guide, *Undertaking Checks and References in Fostering and Adoption Assessments* (Adams, 2017), contains a useful range of forms and a home safety checklist.

Is there sufficient information on the health and safety implications of any pets or other animals, including birds, reptiles or insects which the carers may have? The Good Practice Guide, *Dogs and Pets in Fostering and Adoption* (Adams, 2015), gives useful advice.

Family work patterns

Does the agency have a policy in relation to applicants working outside the home? If applicants do work, how will the needs of children be met if and when they are out of school for any reason? Will young children need to have child care provision away from the foster home? Will the foster carers be available enough to attend reviews and other important meetings and to support the child around contact with their family?

Members of staff

The Guidance does not prohibit a foster carer or a member of their household from also working for the fostering service. However, Guidance 4.12 states that:

> *...care must be taken to avoid any actual or perceived conflict of interest or negative impact on foster children ... for instance, the person may have access to records or may be in a position to influence a placement or approval decision.*

Contact

Fairly high levels of contact with family members are usual for most children placed in foster care. Does the agency have a policy or usual practice of expecting foster carers to transport the child to and from contact, to supervise contact in particular circumstances or to have contact in their own home (this may involve contact with a sibling rather than a parent)? Does the agency have any guidance or procedures for carers on completing records on contact or working on books to provide feedback to parents about their child's development.

Social media and contact

Many children and young people have access to social media, encouraging ways of keeping in touch or finding family members. Does the agency have advice and guidance for foster carers about the safe use of social media and helping children keep in safe contact with their family members? See *Foster Care and Social Networking* (Fursland, 2011).

Allowances

Panel members should be aware of the allowances paid to foster carers. Is a fee also paid? Are there different rates for short-term/emergency carers, long-term carers, family and friends (connected persons) carers? It may be helpful to have information on allowances to keep with this guide.

Long-term fostering (permanence plan)

If a foster carer approved to offer short-term or time-limited care is now offering long-term foster care, it is good practice to undertake an updated assessment. This will include assessing the capacity and skills of the foster carer to provide such a placement. Often this is in relation to a child already placed with them.

For a child to be placed in a long-term foster placement, the child's plan for permanence must be foster care and the foster carer must agree to look after the child until they cease to be looked after. In addition, the responsible authority must confirm the arrangement to the foster carer, the child and anyone with parental responsibility for the child.

The responsible authority can only place a child in a long-term foster placement when certain conditions have been met. It must have prepared a placement plan, ascertained the child's wishes and feelings and given them due consideration, consulted the Independent Reviewing Officer (IRO) and, where appropriate, the child's relatives. The responsible authority must be satisfied that the placement will safeguard and promote the child's welfare and that the foster carer intends to foster the child until they cease to be looked after (see Regulations 22A and 22B of the Care Planning, Placement and Case Review (England) Regulations 2010 (as amended)). The Care Planning, Placement and Case Review Guidance 2015 indicates that the responsible authority must assess the ability of the foster carer to meet the child's needs now and in the future and identify any support services that will be needed to achieve this.

A number of local authorities have already constituted their fostering panels to make recommendations on the suitability of foster carers to provide long-term (permanent) foster care and matches with specific children. It is good practice to consider whether adoption, special guardianship or child arrangements orders have been considered and ruled out for the particular child and foster family. A number of local authorities have developed "certificates" for children where long-term fostering (permanence) is agreed. These provide a special acknowledgement of the permanence plan for the child.

Short break carers

If looked after children are to be placed for more than 24 hours, the carers must be assessed and approved as foster carers. (This is confirmed by Care Planning, Placement and Case Review Guidance 6.13 and 6.14.) What is the agency's policy and practice on short break carers? Do all carers have someone known to them who can provide regular short break care to children in the foster carer's care?

Concurrent or dually-approved carers

These are carers who are dually approved as foster carers and as prospective adopters, more often now being referred to as early permanence carers. They are usually part of a special scheme run by local authorities and/or VAAs, but increasingly local authorities are using dual approval for all their adopters interested in offering early permanence or Fostering for Adoption placements. A child, usually a baby or toddler, can be placed with such a carer on a fostering basis while any work identified with the parents is attempted. If this is not successful, the child, after necessary court and panel involvement, can remain and be adopted by their foster carers.

Often the agency's adoption panel will have been constituted as an adoption and permanence panel to deal with these kind of fostering approvals as well as their adoption work. Otherwise, concurrent carers will need to be considered by both the relevant adoption panel for their approval as prospective adopters and the fostering panel for their approval as foster carers. (See Borthwick and Donnelly, 2013, and Dibben and Howorth, 2017, for more information on concurrent planning.) Does your agency undertake dual approvals, and what is its policy and practice in this area?

Fostering for Adoption

Prospective adopters can be approved as foster carers for a named child where the plan has a very high likelihood of adoption. In these cases, the local authority is able to grant temporary approval under Regulation 25A of the Care Planning, Placement and Case Review (England) Regulations 2010 (as amended). Fostering for Adoption differs from concurrent planning as it is intended for those children where the issues of concern in relation to the birth family are so significant that the local authority has determined that adoption is the likely plan. The child is fostered until, in most cases, work with birth parents, birth family and court involvement enables an adoption plan to be agreed and the child will then be matched with these carers through the adoption panel process (see Fostering for Adoption Practice Guidance 2013, and Dibben and Howorth, 2017).

Annual review

The first annual review of foster carers must be presented to panel. Other annual reviews may be presented, at the discretion of the agency. Does the agency have a policy on whether subsequent reviews are presented? If they are not, how do panel members fulfil their obligation under Regulation 25(4)(a) to monitor the effectiveness of reviews? (See Chapter 6.) Does the agency have guidance for the panel on how it hears reviews?

Representations and complaints

The Children Act 1989 complaints procedure (which is set out in detail in the Children Act 1989 Representations Procedure (England) Regulations 1991) requires local authorities to establish a procedure for considering representations, including complaints. These must be in relation to a specific child. They could include representations about cases that the panel had considered.

Foster carers can make representations, including complaints, to a local authority under the Health and Social Care (Community Health and Standards) Act 2003 if the local authority has a power or duty to provide them with a service. Local authorities do have a general duty to provide services to approved foster carers. Representations would have to be in relation to the service offered (or not offered) and would not be a method of appealing against an agency decision about suitability to foster.

Independent fostering providers are required by Regulation 18 to 'establish a written procedure for considering complaints made by or on behalf of children placed by the agency and foster parents approved by it'.

Panel members should have a copy of the complaints procedure to keep with this guide.

3 Children requiring foster care

The needs of children

The total number of children looked after in England at 31 March 2018 was 75,420 (Department for Education, 2018). Of these children, 73 per cent were in foster placements. The number of looked after children has increased steadily over the last 10 years and continues to do so at a very high rate.

Public and political concern in recent years about the deaths of children as a result of abuse and/or neglect have contributed to a rise in the number of children removed from their birth families and placed in care. Rising numbers of families in poverty and limitations on the availability of preventative and youth services are also likely to have had a significant impact.

More and more children are entering care and many of these are on interim and care orders. It is likely that these children will have suffered or been at risk of suffering abuse and/or neglect within their birth families. In many cases, their parents will have misused drugs and/or alcohol. Many children will have witnessed domestic abuse. Serious parental mental illness may have been a factor. The children and young people in foster care are therefore often very troubled and many are traumatised. Some will have offended; some will be violent; many will have emotional and behavioural difficulties; many will have mental health needs; all will have experienced separation; and many will be grieving significant losses in their lives. (See Aldred and Rodwell, 2018, and Fostering Network's *State of the Nation's Foster Care* report (Lawson and Cann, 2019) for more information.)

There continues to be a national shortage of foster carers. Some children may be placed at a distance from their families or with carers whose skills may not always match the complexity of the children's needs. Children may be transracially and transculturally placed, with families that do not reflect their heritage or language, and may need considerable support. Increasing numbers are unaccompanied asylum-seekers. Children and young people who are lesbian, gay, non-binary or transgender may need support and skilled care.

Also, children and young people with mental health difficulties may be placed with carers who do not have the requisite skills, knowledge and support. Disabled children, requiring support, may be placed with families with little experience of caring for a disabled child. Foster families are needed who can face and deal appropriately with these challenges. They need resilience, commitment, compassion and high levels of support and training.

Many children and young people in foster care return to live with members of their birth family. There will have been regular contact between the child in foster care and the birth family. Some will often keep in touch through social media and this can be challenging and complex. An assessment will have been undertaken with the birth family and ongoing family support will usually be offered to the child and family once reunited. However, the plans for children in foster care can change or be delayed. Sometimes not enough time is devoted to enabling children to return home or to other alternative permanent placements. Government targets have been set to reduce the number of moves children experience in care and to reinforce the stability of continuous care in one placement.

Furthermore, the Government expects that permanence will be considered for all children at their four-month review, following entry into care. This means that reunification with the parents, placement with family and friends, adoption, long-term fostering, independent living and residential placements as permanent arrangements need to be considered and planned by local authorities. This is reinforced in the Care Planning, Placement and Case Review (England) Regulations 2010 (as amended) and in the Children and Families Act 2014, which sets out that care proceedings should be concluded within 26 weeks. There is huge pressure in the system.

It is important that fostering service providers ensure that panel members are provided with information about the profile of children and foster carers in their areas so that members are then in a position to consider fostering assessments relative to the specific needs of children.

Child-focused service

The recent Government report, *Fostering Better Outcomes* (Department for Education, 2018), and the Fostering Network's *State of the Nation's Foster Care* report (Lawson and Cann, 2019) emphasise the challenging and key role played by foster carers within a foster care service. They reinforce that carers have a central role as part of the team around the child, both in terms of the care of the child and in contributing to plans and services needed by the child. Foster carers should be viewed and treated as good, responsible and reasonable parents who, with delegated authority, are able to make many day-to-day decisions about the child in line with the placement plan, e.g. agreeing to sleepovers, etc. Children need to live in foster families where they do not stand out and where their experience is normalised. The NMS set out the requirements to be met in order to achieve the best outcomes for children in foster care (see child-focused standards 1–12). The NMS also set out the key values as underpinning principles (see Appendix 1). These standards and outcomes are ones that panel members should bear in mind when considering the approval of foster carers or plans for matches with children.

Permanence plans for children

Long-term fostering

As previously stated, a plan for permanence has to be considered for every looked after child. For a significant number of those children, the plan will be long-term fostering. This may be a long-term fostering placement with their existing foster carers, or with new foster carers, where careful matching should have taken place. There will also be some children where the plan will be long-term fostering with family and friends as approved foster carers.

Guidance is given on permanence planning in Care Planning, Placement and Case Review Guidance 2.3–2.6. It states that 'the objective of planning for permanence is…to ensure that children have a secure, stable and loving family to support them throughout childhood and beyond'. As stated in the previous chapter, arrangements and conditions for making long-term fostering placements are set out in the Care Planning, Placement and Case Review (England) Regulations 2010 (as amended).

Long-term fostering can work well for many children, and offer them a "sense of permanence". Children in long-term placements can maintain contact with birth family members and have a real sense of belonging to their foster family. Many placements may benefit from the continuing statutory involvement of the local authority as this can ensure that support services are provided. It should be noted, however, that the carers do not gain parental responsibility for the child; the child remains a looked after child and is therefore subject to continuing statutory reviews and social work involvement. There is provision for visits to be less frequent, and meetings as part of a review may be held once-yearly. Long-term fostering needs very careful consideration and good practice would suggest that there is sufficient exploration of the range of legal options open to carers who wish to undertake this task.

Special guardianship

Some carers, including family and friends (connected persons) carers, may choose to apply to a court for an order called special guardianship, under the Children Act 1989 as amended by the Adoption and Children Act 2002. This offers an alternative legal status for children. The child is no longer looked after. The order gives the special guardian parental responsibility, which they can exercise to the exclusion of others. It is important to note that the parent/s retain parental responsibility but their exercise of it is restricted. The local authority has a duty to assess the support needs of special guardians where children have been looked after and financial support can be payable to previous foster carers of children. The prescribed support services are very similar to those provided for adopters. Carers may choose to apply for special guardianship orders but in many cases they will need to be sure of the support services on offer before considering such applications.

Child arrangements order

Child arrangements orders replace residence and contact orders. They regulate arrangements about when and with whom the child is to live, spend time or otherwise have contact. They are made in private proceedings. Some carers may consider applying for these.

Adoption

In some long-term arrangements, carers may decide to apply to adopt the child or young person. An adoption order is made under the Adoption and Children Act 2002. An adoption order confers full parental responsibility on the adoptive parents. Support services are on offer and the local authority or relevant RAA has a duty to assess these if it arranges the adoption. Carers may receive financial support. Foster carers would usually need to be assessed and approved as adopters by an adoption agency before an adoption can proceed. However, foster carers who have had a child in their care for a year can apply to adopt the child without the agreement of the local authority and without being approved as adopters. The decision will be made by the court. See Dibben and Howorth (2016) for more information about adoption by foster carers.

Remit of the panel in permanence planning

There are no legal requirements for long-term fostering plans for children to be considered by a panel. However, given the potential life-long significance of the plan for the child and the family concerned, such matters are often referred to the local authority's fostering panel. The panel will be asked to recommend a permanent match between the child and the family.

In such cases, it is important that the panel bears in mind the possibility of adoption for children when permanence plans are being made. The panel may, therefore, not always recommend that long-term fostering is in the child's best interests. Should adoption be considered a more appropriate plan, this would need to be referred back to the relevant local authority for consideration and a court order.

Information required in recommending permanent matches

In considering matches for long-term or permanent fostering, the panel would require not only the assessment report on the foster carers, but also a report about the child and a matching report outlining why this match is appropriate.

The panel members would need to consider the ability of the proposed family to meet the child or young person's needs, both now and in the future; to take into account the views of all members of the foster family; to consider the views of the child or young person and birth family members about the plan; and to advise on the contact arrangements with the birth family, as well as the support needs and support services that would be provided to the family.

The child's social worker and the foster carers' supervising or assessing social worker should present the matter to panel. The carer should also be invited to attend the panel meeting and the panel should reach its recommendation in its usual way (see section on reaching the recommendation in Chapter 4).

4 Considering the approval of foster carers

The panel's legal functions

The fostering panel's primary legal function is to make recommendations about the approval of foster carers. It is therefore not possible for the fostering service provider to accomplish some of its work without first referring matters to the fostering panel for a recommendation to be made. The legal functions include the following under Regulation 25(1) of the Regulations.

(a) to consider each application for approval and to recommend whether or not a person is suitable to be a foster parent,

(b) where it recommends approval of an application, to recommend any terms on which the approval is to be given…

This means that fostering service providers must ensure that the fostering panel considers and makes a recommendation about approval of foster carers before proceeding to make a decision and then placing children. The only exceptions to this relate to local authority fostering service providers who can place a child with a "connected person", i.e. a relative, friend or other person connected with the child, for up to 16 weeks without reference to a fostering panel – Care Planning, Placement and Case Review (England) Regulations 2010, Regulation 24. This is considered in more detail in Chapter 5. A local authority can also grant temporary approval as a foster carer to a prospective adopter for a named child under Regulation 25A of the Care Planning, Placement and Case Review (England) Regulations 2010.

The panel's role: messages from Serious Case Reviews

The vast majority of children in foster care are provided with safe family placements but in a significant number of cases, children across the UK experience harm each year from those responsible for their care. In a small number of very serious cases involving the persistent neglect, emotional and/or sexual abuse of children, it was clear that the foster carers concerned should never have been recruited. High quality assessment, recruitment and review procedures are therefore needed to prevent these individuals being able to harm children (see *Croydon Serious Case Review*, Griffin, 2016). These procedures should include the role and function of fostering panels. Panels need to be fair, challenging and robust.

Assessments of foster carers

A number of principles of good practice should apply in considering the approval of foster carers. Firstly, the fostering panel has a primary responsibility to act in the best interests of children and young people placed in foster care. Secondly, the panel must consider an assessment report about the prospective foster carers. Thirdly, the process should be conducted in a fair and transparent way. NMS 13 covers the recruitment and assessment of foster carers. The Regulations set out the assessment and approval process (Regulations 26 and 27).

There are two Stages to the assessment process. Stage 1 requires the collection of basic information about the applicant in accordance with Regulation 26(1A). This requires the fostering service to obtain particular information specified in Part 1 of Schedule 3 to the Regulations, make other checks and request references. Through the gathering of this basic information, it is intended that any applicants who are found to be clearly unsuitable can be sifted out at this point. Stage 2 involves a more detailed assessment in accordance with Regulation 26(2). This requires the fostering service to obtain the information about the applicant as set out in Part 2 of Schedule 3. Stages 1 and 2 can run concurrently.

STAGE 1

Checks and references

- Apart from gathering factual information about the applicant and the household, a number of Stage 1 checks and references are required.

These are set out fully in the Guidance and in the Prospective Foster Carer Report (Form F) England 2018 (produced by CoramBAAF), and in the Good Practice Guide, *Undertaking Checks and References in Fostering and Adoption Assessments* (Adams, 2017). The Prospective Foster Carer Report is widely used. Checks and references include health details supported by medical reports, household accommodation including a health and safety assessment, local authority checks, personal references, and DBS checks. If the applicant has been a foster carer within the last 12 months, approved by another fostering service provider, that provider must be asked for a reference. Otherwise, if the applicant has been an approved foster carer or adopter, their previous agency or fostering service may be contacted for access to records, and where the applicant consents; it is good practice to do so. The Guidance states that:

> *Any information about a foster carer's conduct or suitability to foster that has caused concern should be shared, even if the individual has refused consent.*

Enhanced DBS checks

The Regulations require that enhanced Disclosure and Barring Service (DBS) checks are carried out on prospective foster carers and on all members of their household aged 18 and over. (Some fostering agencies may require checks on people of 16 and over.) An enhanced disclosure means that a list will be provided of any convictions or cautions, and any reprimands or warnings that were issued when the applicant was a juvenile. The police may also choose to disclose information thought to be relevant, often referred to as "soft intelligence". This may include information about an unsubstantiated allegation or dismissal from a job where there were concerns about conduct towards a child (see City and Hackney Serious Case Review, quoted in Adams, 2017, p11). People are automatically regarded as unsuitable to become foster carers if they have convictions or cautions for certain specified offences and should not be taken further through the assessment process. Broadly speaking, these are offences against children. For children placed with family or friends and existing foster carers, there can be exemptions from this. In such cases, the welfare of the child is always paramount. Legal advice should be sought and a senior manager should be involved in any decision to exercise discretion in particular circumstances. (See Regulation 26(8) and Guidance 5.33 and 5.34 for full details.)

Apart from automatic exclusions, panels need to take into account any offences that may have been committed and consider the implications of these for the fostering of children and young people. Questions to explore include the age, type and seriousness of the offences, the prospective foster carer's honesty in informing the fostering service provider, their age at the time, their attitude towards the offences now, and whether the foster carer is a relative or already a foster carer for the child. The overriding consideration is always what is in the best interests of children.

Health assessment

Details of the prospective foster carer's health are required, supported by a medical report. This is usually completed on the Adult Health form (Form AH, CoramBAAF) by the applicant's GP. The agency medical adviser will evaluate this, gather more information if required, and provide written advice about the health of the applicants.

Local authority checks

Agencies must seek any relevant information held by the local authority where the applicants live. This should include information from social care records, including child protection, and from education records. Good practice would suggest that checks should also be done with previous local authorities where applicants have resided. Usually the last 10 years are covered. It may also be helpful to do a check with a local authority where the applicant has jointly parented children with a previous partner.

Personal references

Unless a fostering service provider for whom the applicant has fostered in the preceding 12 months provides a reference, there must be written reports on interviews with at least two personal referees. Good practice would suggest that these should not be related to the applicant. It is helpful if, between them, referees have known each applicant for a considerable period of time, as well as still being in close touch. For some applicants, it may be necessary to have information from more than the specified number of referees to achieve this. It can also be helpful to have a reference from a relative in each partner's family, rather than from just one side of the family.

At any point during Stage 1, if the fostering service's decision-maker decides that the applicant is not suitable to foster, they must write to the applicant informing them of this decision and give full reasons for it. At the very latest, the fostering service must make a decision about whether to proceed within 10 days of gathering all the Stage 1 information. The applicant has no right to make written representations to the decision-maker or to apply to the Independent Review Mechanism (IRM).

STAGE 2

The Stage 2 assessment is detailed and will explore the applicant's family background and childhood, their adult life, their personality and current relationship, household members (including children), lifestyle and support network. The assessment of the applicant's fostering capacity to care for children will then be carefully evaluated and evidenced (see Prospective Foster Carer's Report (Form F) England, CoramBAAF, 2018).

Further checks and references

Further checks, references and verification of documents will also be undertaken in Stage 2. These will usually include, as appropriate: current employer and volunteer activity references; previous employment and volunteer activity references where the applicant worked with children or vulnerable adults; ex-partners; adult children; a financial assessment; completion of pets and animals questionnaires; school, college and nursery checks; and a social media check.

Ex-partners and adult children

It is good practice to have a reference from any adult children of either applicant. It can also be helpful to have a reference from a former partner of either applicant, particularly if there has been joint parenting experience with the applicant. However, even if they have not parented together, a former partner may be well placed to comment on an applicant's personality and behaviour (Adams, 2017). Agencies and panel members need to be clear what their policy is on this. Some ex-partners may be very bitter and still angry, and what they say must be considered in this context. It will be important to try to check any negative comments against the comments of adult children and/or personal referees. Where an applicant refuses to give information that would allow the agency to contact an ex-partner, they should be asked to give reasons for this, e.g. that the ex-partner is violent and might pose a serious threat. As far as possible, these need to be checked and verified by any adult children, referees or by external agencies, e.g. GP or the police. The agency and panel members will then need to make a judgement as to whether the lack of contact with an ex-partner is crucial to the consideration of the applicants or not.

Financial assessment

There is no requirement that an applicant has a minimum standard of income. As Adams (2017) sets out, it is important to be confident that an applicant is responsible about managing their money and in a good position, financially, to foster. It must be clear that a placement will not disrupt due to a financial crisis like non-payment of rent or mortgage and that the carer will not need to use the fostering allowance to cover their general household expenses. It is also important that carers are not unduly stressed by financial difficulties. It will be important therefore to check that the financial assessment and implications have been carefully thought through and evidenced.

Applicants who may have lived abroad for extended periods

Agencies should consider taking up checks and references where applicants may have lived abroad. Some agencies have found that contact with a local police authority in the country concerned has produced helpful information or confirmation that the applicant was not known. An employer's reference covering the period may also be helpful.

Internet and social media

Over recent years, many more people have become regular users of the internet and social media. There is therefore potentially information held about people on the internet, some of it public and some private. It is now advised that agencies undertake an internet check, with an applicant's consent. Such a check may reveal important information affecting whether an applicant is considered suitable to care for children. (See Practice Note 55, *Using the Internet in Adoption and Fostering Assessments* (BAAF, 2015) for more information.)

Brief reports

If, at some point during Stage 2, the agency decides that the applicant is unlikely to be suitable to foster and they do not wish to withdraw, a brief report may be prepared and submitted to the fostering panel. The applicant must be notified that the brief report is to be sent to the panel, provided with a copy of it, and given 10 working days to send their observations. The panel is then asked to make a recommendation to the fostering service decision-maker. Under Regulation 25 (2A) of the Regulations the fostering panel must either:

(a) request the fostering service provider to prepare a further written report, covering all the matters set out in regulation 26 (2)(c); or

(b) recommend that the person is not suitable to be a foster parent.

If the proposed decision is that the person is not suitable, called a "qualifying determination", the applicant may, within 28 days, make representations to the decision-maker or apply to the Independent Review Mechanism (IRM). If representations are received, the matter must be referred back to the panel before a final decision is made. If the case is referred to the IRM, their recommendation, as well as that of the original fostering panel, must be taken into account before a final decision is made (Regulation 27).

The full assessment report

The assessment report covering suitability of prospective foster carers must contain the information required in Schedule 3 of the regulations and any other information considered relevant by the fostering service provider. This information should include a written medical report and Form AH (Adult Health) should have been completed.

Many fostering service providers are using an evidence-based assessment model that requires prospective foster carers to provide evidence of their abilities to undertake the necessary tasks required. Evidence of fostering capacity should be assessed. This includes: the capacity to care for children, providing warmth, empathy and encouragement; the ability to provide structure and boundaries; the ability to provide durability, resilience and commitment; being able to work effectively with others; and having understanding of identity and diversity. Motivation to foster, preparation, training, anticipated impact of fostering and understanding of safer caring should also be outlined.

The NMS outline a number of important standards for assessments. NMS 1–12 are child-focused standards that set out what children in foster care need from their carers.

Furthermore, NMS 13.3 requires that:

Prospective foster carers are prepared to become foster carers in a way which addresses and gives practical techniques to manage the issues they are likely to encounter and identifies the competencies and strengths they have or need to develop.

NMS 13.4 states:

The assessment process is set out clearly to prospective foster carers, including:

- *the qualities, skills or aptitudes being sought or to be achieved*
- *the standards to be applied in the assessment*
- *the stages and content of the selection process and the timescales involved*
- *the information to be given to applicants*

NMS 13.6 requires that:

Prospective foster carers are considered in terms of their capacity to look after children in a safe and responsible way that meets the child's developmental needs.

Issues to be covered will include:

- child rearing
- caring for children born to someone else
- contact between fostered children and their families
- helping children make sense of their past

- sexual boundaries and attitudes
- awareness of issues around child abuse
- approaches to discipline
- awareness of how to promote secure attachments between children and appropriate adults
- awareness of own motivation for fostering/own needs to be met through the fostering process
- religion
- ethnicity/cultural/linguistic issues
- standard of living and lifestyle
- health
- own experience of parenting and being parented
- own experiences in relation to disability and/or attitudes to disability

Some agencies also refer to the Secure Base Model (Schofield and Beek, 2014) in undertaking the assessment and completing an analysis of the applicant's capacity to meet the needs of children. The Secure Base Model is already incorporated into the Skills to Foster Preparation training programme, which the applicant will have attended (Fostering Network, 2009, 2014). The model is drawn from attachment theory and proposes the following five dimensions of caregiving, which overlap with each other to create a secure base for the child: availability (helping the child to trust); sensitivity (helping the child to manage feelings); acceptance (building the child's self-esteem); co-operative caregiving (helping the child to feel effective); and family membership (helping the child to belong). See Schofield and Beek, 2014 and www.uea.ac.uk/providingasecurebase.

Where relevant, the assessor may include additional assessment reports covering parent and child fostering, long-term or permanent fostering, or other specialist fostering schemes.

All supporting information to the main report should be documented and much of this should be made available to panel members.

Social work analysis and terms of approval

In concluding the report, the assessing social worker will need to provide an analysis of the prospective foster carer's strengths, limitations, abilities and areas for development. The report should also include proposals about the terms and conditions of any approval. This should include the age range, numbers of children and type of fostering approval recommended. Any restrictions or conditions should also be specified. Open approvals for very wide-spanning age groups in all matching consideration categories should be considered very carefully and evidence provided of the capacity of carers to meet the needs of children in such a range.

It is not necessary to specify gender in the approval terms except where there is a clear preference stated by the applicant. For most applicants, caring for children and young people of any gender, including trans young people, should have been explored in the assessment and the panel will need to be satisfied that this has been undertaken (See CoramBAAF, 2018b).

It should be noted that Schedule 7 to the Children Act 1989 limits the number of children who may be fostered by a foster carer to the 'usual fostering limit' of three children unless all children placed are one sibling group. An exemption to this limit may be granted by the area local authority in which the foster carer lives. Nevertheless, the foster carer's terms of approval need to allow it. The Guidance sets out that any terms of approval must be compatible with the number of children the foster carer can care for even if an exemption to the usual fostering limit has been granted, unless the placement is in an emergency and for less than six days. Clearly the terms of approval must make sense in terms of the assessment and reflect the evidence of suitability and capacity to foster.

Guidance 5.22 states, in relation to foster carers, that:

> *Subject to the need to protect children and deal sensitively with third party information, they should be able to read in advance any reports concerning them which are being presented to the panel and to make any further written submission themselves.*

Panel members' responsibilities

The panel's role is to examine either a brief report or a full assessment report and to consider whether there is evidence of an applicant's abilities and suitability to foster. A "panel member notes sheet" attached to each case can help members prepare their views and consider areas for clarification (see Appendix 9 for an example). Before making recommendations to the fostering service provider, essential questions for panel members should include the following:

- Have the statutory checks been undertaken and are these satisfactory?

- Have at least two personal referees been interviewed and written reports of interviews provided? Do the referees adequately cover both applicants, if a couple? Have they known the family over a number of years? Should more references be taken up, including from a family member?

- If the applicant was previously married or in a long-term significant relationship, has a reference been taken up from the ex-partner? If not, why not?

- Have the applicant's own children by birth and any other children permanently in the household been interviewed? If not, why not?

- Has a chronology of the applicant's life been provided? Is there sufficient independent verification of the applicant's chronology and any self-reported information?

- Does the report include an analysis of the information provided by the assessing social worker with clear recommendations of the range and terms of approval?

- Has sufficient evidence of fostering capacity been provided?

- Is there evidence of their ability to work effectively with others?

- Have areas for future development and support been identified?

- Does the applicant provide evidence of anti-discriminatory and anti-racist approaches to parenting?

- Do they have a good support network?

- Can the applicant meet the National Minimum Standards (Standards 1–12) or could they be supported to do so?

- Do the terms of approval appear appropriate given the assessed abilities of the prospective foster carer(s), the suitability of the household and the needs of children in the age group recommended?

Questions from children and young people

A number of agencies have consulted with looked after children and young people regarding questions they would like to ask of prospective foster carers. It is suggested that the panel asks one or two of the questions suggested. Examples may include:

- What would you do if a child was sad?

- What would you say to a child about why you want to foster?

- How would a child or young person know if you are a cheerful or happy person?

- How would they know that they were safe in your home?

- What are your expectations of a young person, bearing in mind that they say they don't really care?

- How would they know what to expect in how you use discipline?

(Adapted from Fosterplus' consultation with young people, 2015)

Attending the panel

NMS 14.5 requires that:

Foster carers and prospective foster carers are given the opportunity to attend and be heard at all panel meetings at which their approval is being discussed and to bring a supporter to the panel if they wish.

Guidance 5.22 confirms this. This enables prospective carers to meet panel members and make any direct observations they wish about the assessment and their application. This also gives panel members the opportunity to ask direct questions of prospective carers. The attendance of prospective foster carers at the panel is a tangible demonstration of working in partnership with the agency. This is reinforced by the IRM's Annual Report, June 2018. This emphasises that fostering panels need to be transparent. It notes, though, that where panels are considering third party information, they will need to do this without foster carers present. However, the IRM can see no reason why foster carers cannot be present with social workers for the rest of the time. The IRM acknowledges that panels will need time for discussion but this should be without the applicant or presenting social workers.

Attendance can be daunting for the applicants, however, and every effort should be made to put people at their ease. Good preparation of prospective foster carers is essential. Training should be provided for panel members to assist the development of their skills in managing this process.

Sometimes prospective carers are unable to attend in person due to distance or other issues. This should not negate their participation and creative and accessible alternatives should be considered. For example, they could be invited to participate through the use of telephone or video conferencing, e.g. Skype.

Usual practice involves panel members preparing their questions prior to the attendance of the social worker and foster carer applicants. The Chair may provide a short factual summary of the application. Both strengths and issues of concern should be identified. The Chair then introduces themself and explains the panel process to the prospective foster carer(s) outside of the panel meeting. The Chair may inform them of the areas that will be raised. The social worker may occasionally attend initially on their own if the panel members wish to examine particular issues first (e.g. concerns raised by referees or other third parties). The social worker and prospective foster carer(s) then attend for questions and observations. Questions may be raised through the Chair or by individual panel members. Prospective foster carer(s) and the social worker then usually leave the meeting. Exceptionally, the social worker may remain to address any further points. The social worker should then leave the meeting. The panel then deliberates and reaches its recommendation. The Chair then immediately informs the prospective foster carer(s) of the recommendation and explains the decision-making process. This may take place in the panel meeting or in the waiting room. The panel discussion is recorded, including the reasons for its recommendation (Regulation 24(2)).

It is important to consider how much weight is given to the attendance and performance of prospective foster carers at the panel. Panels need to be wary as to how people perform in particular circumstances and there may be a tendency to over- or under-compensate or make judgements on this basis. Panels need to be mindful of not making judgements based on first impressions – the weight of evidence as to whether people should be approved as foster carers should be provided in the assessment report. Nevertheless, if people appear very significantly different from the report provided, this may require more investigation.

Feedback should be gathered from prospective foster carers and presenting social workers as to their experience of attending the panel so that the panel can evaluate its own performance and make any necessary changes.

Reaching a recommendation

As previously stated, fostering panels are required to make recommendations to fostering service providers. The panel can do one of three things:

- make a positive recommendation;
- make a negative recommendation;
- defer making a recommendation in order for further information to be made available.

There are two stages involved in panel members reaching a recommendation.

Prior to attending the panel meeting

Panel members will need to do the following.

- Consider and take into account the report sent to them. NMS 14.3 requires that 'all necessary information is provided to panel members at least five working days in advance of the panel meeting to enable full and proper consideration'.
- Make a note of questions the panel member may wish to clarify at the meeting regarding the application.
- Highlight any information that the member believes to be missing.
- Identify strengths and vulnerabilities in the assessment report as the panel member perceives it, using the panel member notes sheet, if provided.

During the panel meeting

At the meeting itself, panel members will discuss together their questions and comments about the reports and prepare themselves for considering the application as a panel. They will consider any suggested questions provided by children and young people. The panel Chair has a very significant role at this point. It is important that each panel member has an opportunity to ask questions or make comments on every issue. The Chair may facilitate this by asking each member in turn for their questions and comments, starting with a different person each time. Alternatively, the Chair may check with everyone that their questions and comments have been considered.

The presenting workers and applicants or carers will then be invited into the meeting to respond to the questions posed. As stated above, many panels ask applicants and presenting social workers to leave the panel whilst they formulate their recommendation.

Reaching a recommendation as to the suitability of an applicant to become a foster carer needs careful and rigorous consideration. It is essential that children are placed with families that can safeguard and promote their welfare.

Once the panel is ready to reach its recommendation, each panel member should be asked whether they support the proposed recommendation. Where panel members have serious reservations, the Chair should ensure that these are recorded in the minutes of the panel's meetings and are also attached to the panel's recommendations. Recommended practice is that the Chair summarises each recommendation made and the reasons for it, as well as any dissenting views, with reasons, during the meeting. It is essential that the panel is also clear about the recommended terms of approval. It is critically important that the decision-maker for the fostering service is aware of not only the recommendation and the reasons behind it but also of any dissenting views.

If a panel is evenly split, it is not in a position to make a positive recommendation. If, however, there is a majority in favour of the recommendation, the panel can proceed to reach a positive recommendation. The views of dissenting panel members should be clearly minuted.

The panel Chair does not have a casting vote as all members are equally responsible for forming a view on the case. (However, the Chair of an adoption panel does have a casting vote, so where an adoption panel, including the Chair, is evenly split, the Chair's view prevails. Panels that make both adoption and fostering recommendations will need to be aware of this difference.)

Sometimes important and relevant information is not available in the paperwork and panel members are unable to reach a recommendation. They should therefore defer making a recommendation and make clear to the presenting social workers what additional information is needed. A date should be set if at all possible for the case to return to panel. No recommendation is made and the matter is not referred to the fostering service provider decision-maker.

It is, however, important that deferring making a recommendation is not in fact an excuse for not coming to a conclusion when information is available. All panel members should work hard to reach a view. Abstentions are not appropriate or helpful. It is always the safeguarding and promotion of welfare of children that must be the primary focus of the recommendation made.

Approvals – decision-making process

The fostering service provider is responsible for deciding whether to approve a person as a foster carer (see CoramBAAF, 2019). Guidance 5.39 specifies that 'the fostering service must identify a senior member of staff who will receive the panel's recommendations and make decisions as required. More than one decision-maker may be appointed but they may not delegate their authority to another person.' NMS 23.12 requires that the decision-maker 'is a senior person within the fostering service, or is a trustee or director of the fostering service who is a social worker with at least three years' post-qualifying experience in childcare social work and has knowledge of childcare law and practice'. Where there are joint panels, each agency should have its own decision-maker. The Regulations lay down that no person on the panel can take part in any decision made by a fostering service provider. Regulation 27(3) and (4) states that:

(3) A fostering service provider must, in deciding whether to approve X as a foster parent and as to the terms of any approval, take into account the recommendation of its fostering panel.

(4) No member of the fostering panel may take part in any decision made by a fostering service provider under paragraph (3).

In complex cases, the decision-maker may want to clarify points with the Chair or agency adviser. The Chair must always be mindful that they cannot take part in the decision or appear to be doing so. Guidance 5.23 confirms that:

Since no member of the fostering panel is permitted to take part in deciding to approve a person as a foster carer, the panel Chair will not be in a position to discuss the case with the decision-maker and the recommendations should be passed on by way of the written minutes of the panel meeting setting out the main points of discussion and reasons for the recommendation.

NMS 14.9 requires the decision-maker:

…to take account of the panel's recommendation and all other information available to them. They must make a decision within seven working days of receipt of the recommendation and final set of panel minutes.

Guidance 5.40 (as amended) quotes case law guidance on how the decision-maker should approach a case. (See Decision Forms in Appendix 3.)

It is essential that the decision-maker examines the arguments and considerations set out in the assessment and is satisfied that the panel process has been fair and rigorous. The decision-maker needs to be clear that they have taken account of the panel's recommendation and reasons, and considered any additional material before proceeding to make their decision, if positive. Their decision may be different to the recommendation made by the panel. It is very important that the decision-maker sets out their own reasons for their decision and does not simply provide an endorsement of the panel's recommendation and its reasons (See IRM Annual Report, June 2018, and CoramBAAF, 2019).

Should the decision-maker decide to approve, they must write to the applicant specifying the terms of approval and enter into a foster care agreement as outlined in Schedule 5 to the Regulations. Panels should be informed of all decisions made.

Qualifying determinations and representations – decision-making process

Should the decision-maker have concerns about an applicant's suitability to foster, they may make a qualifying determination that the applicant should not be approved. As above, when making positive decisions, the decision-maker should take account of the panel's recommendation and follow the same rigorous process before making a qualifying determination (see qualifying determination form in Appendix 3). They should then proceed in the following way under Regulation 27(6):

(a) give X written notice that they propose not to approve X as suitable to be foster parent (a 'qualifying determination'), together with their reasons and a copy of the fostering panel's recommendation; and

(b) advise X that, within 28 days of the date of the qualifying determination X may –

   (i) submit any written representations that X wishes to make to the fostering service provider, or

   (ii) apply to the Secretary of State for a review by an independent review panel of the qualifying determination.

- Written notice should be sent via recorded delivery.
- If no representations are received, and the applicant does not apply to the IRM, the decision-maker may proceed to make their decision (Regulation 27(8)).
- If written representations are received within 28 days, the decision-maker must then refer the case to the fostering panel for further consideration (Regulation 27(9)(a)). As in the assessment process, the applicants must be invited to attend the panel meeting in part to discuss their written representation. Applicants should be free to provide any further information they wish, and to bring a supporter to panel (NMS 14.5). The assessing social worker and their manager will also be asked

to attend. There will need to be regard to the requirements under the GDPR and DPA 2018, should a supporter attend (see Adams and Jordan, 2019).

Following this, the panel makes its recommendation, taking into account the representation. This recommendation is a fresh one. It may uphold a previous recommendation but it has to take account of the representation. The decision-maker can then make their decision, taking into account the panel's fresh recommendation (Regulation 27(8)(b)).

In cases where the applicant has applied to the IRM, this will be dealt with by the IRM, currently operated by Coram Children's Legal Centre under contract to the Department for Education. IRM panels are set up and operate in a similar way to agency panels. They receive reports, meet the applicants and social workers, and make a recommendation. This is then considered by the decision-maker before they make the final decision. When carers are being considered for the first time, they can only apply to the IRM if there is a qualifying determination that they are not suitable to foster. They are not able to apply at this stage (but are subsequently – see Chapter 6) if they are deemed suitable but the terms of their approval, i.e. age and/or number of children, are not what they want.

As soon as practicable after making the decision, the fostering service provider must write to the prospective foster carer either notifying the terms of approval and entering into a foster care agreement under Schedule 5 or explaining the reasons for deciding not to approve. This should be done in a timely manner, as long delays are unhelpful and often unnecessary. There is no further right of appeal.

It is important to note that foster carers can only be approved by one fostering service provider at any one time and their application must have been considered by the fostering panel for that fostering service provider.

Range of fostering tasks

The range of fostering tasks provided by foster carers include the following types:

- **short-term/time-limited foster care** where children and young people are likely to return to their family, be bridged to adoption or to other placements, be bridged to independence, etc.;
- **short break (respite care)** where children and young people, including disabled children, may be looked after for short breaks as a support to birth or other foster families and residential placements;
- **supportive lodgings** for young people in the 16 plus age range;
- **remand and intensive lodgings** for young people who are offending;
- **parent and child placements** for assessment and support;
- **specialist schemes** for particularly challenging children needing therapeutic placements;
- **early permanence placements** in which children may be reunited with their birth family or may be adopted by their foster/concurrency carers;
- **long-term or permanent fostering** for children and young people who have a plan for permanence in foster care (see Chapter 3 for more information).

5 Family and friends as foster carers (connected persons)

There is now much better recognition of the value of making placements with extended family or friends for looked after children. Moreover, it is known that children in such placements often do best across a range of measures. There is a duty under the Children Act 1989 for a local authority to consider this (see Chapter 3). It is estimated that around 200,000 children in the UK are being raised by family and friends because their parents are unable to care for them. The vast majority of these family and friends carers look after children in informal arrangements or through a variety of legal orders. Of these, 79 per cent are grandparents, 76 per cent are between the ages of 45–64 years, and 15 per cent are over 65 years (see the Grandparents Plus report, *Kinship Care: State of the Nation 2018*, Mervyn-Smith, 2018). Around 18 per cent of all children in foster care in England are placed with family and friends who are approved as foster carers.

The advantages are clear – there is often an established relationship with the child; the continuity of ethnic and cultural heritage may be maintained; the trauma of separation is reduced; and such placements can be more stable in the long term. Difficulties are reported, however, by family and friends carers. These commonly include coping with a child's emotional and behavioural difficulties, and complex dynamics in contact arrangements with parents. Many carers have also highlighted the need for better support, emotionally, practically and financially (see Farmer and Moyers, 2008; Hunt *et al*, 2008; and Mervyn-Smith, 2018).

The Government published *Family and Friends Care: Statutory guidance for local authorities* (DfE, 2011). This sets out a framework for family and friends carers, whatever the legal status of the child they are caring for. It requires each local authority in England with responsibility for children's services, in collaboration with local partners, to publish a policy setting out its approach towards meeting the needs of children living with family and friends carers.

Children may be living with family or friends as carers in a variety of different arrangements. It is important to know the route by which the child is placed with the family or friend. The Regulations apply only in situations where the local authority has placed a looked after child with family and friends. The Fostering Services Statutory Guidance, NMS 30, Care Planning, Placement and Case Review (England) Regulations 2010 and Guidance 2015 also deal with these placements.

The Family and Friends Guidance defines a "connected person" as a relative, friend or other person connected with a looked after child. A "family and friends carer" is a relative, friend or other person connected with someone else's child who is caring for that child full time. The child may or may not be looked after by a local authority. A connected person will also be a family and friends carer if they are looking after the child full time.

Arrangements for the care of children

Informal arrangements

Many children may be living with close family members under informal arrangements made within the family. These do not require intervention by the local authority, and the relatives caring for the child are not approved as foster carers. The child is not looked after. The relatives may receive support from the local authority under section 17 of the Children Act 1989, which allows the local authority to provide support to children in need.

Private fostering

A number of children live with friends or distant relatives under a private arrangement. As the carers are not close relatives (i.e. not the child's brother, sister, uncle, aunt or grandparent), they are private foster carers and the Children (Private Arrangements for Fostering) Regulations 2005 apply. Under the Children Act 1989, the child is privately fostered when with the carer for 28 days or more. The private foster carers are required to inform the local authority that they are privately fostering a child, and a social worker should visit on a regular basis. Private foster carers are not approved as foster carers like those approved by fostering service providers under the 2011 Regulations.

Special guardianship

A family member or friend may apply to obtain a special guardianship order in respect of a child for whom they are caring. This is an order under the Children Act 1989. The child is no longer looked after. It gives the special guardian parental responsibility which they can exercise to the exclusion of others. The birth parent/s retain parental responsibility. Support services, including financial support, can be provided by local authorities. There has been a considerable increase over recent years in the number of children who have left care through special guardianship orders made to family and friends carers.

Child arrangements order

A child arrangements order will specify when and with whom a child will live and when and with whom a child will spend time or otherwise have contact. A family member or friend may apply for a child arrangements order if they have a residence or contact order, if the child has lived with them for at least 12 months or if they have leave of the court to make such an application.

Adoption

In a small number of cases, a family member or friend may adopt a child for whom they have been caring. This transfers full parental responsibility to them.

Fostering a specific looked after child

Extended family members and friends may put themselves forward to care for or be asked to care for a specific child who is looked after by the local authority. As it is the local authority that decides to place the child with the relative or friend, the family or friend carer will need to be approved as a local authority foster carer. In these situations, the fostering panel will be required to make a recommendation as to their suitability as foster carers. If the placement is a planned one, it would be possible for the prospective carer to be assessed and approved by an independent fostering provider, although this is unusual.

Family and Friends Care Statutory Guidance 5.16 states that:

> Standard 30 of the NMS clarifies that when a foster carer is being assessed for approval for a specific child or children only, there is no need to consider their suitability to care for other children. NMS 30.3 states that the decision on approval must take into account the needs, wishes and feelings of the child and the capacity of the carer to meet these.

Assessments are often undertaken using CoramBAAF's Form C.

Simmonds (2011) suggests that any assessments of family and friends as carers should be conducted:

- *in a spirit of enquiry;*
- *in a spirit of partnership;*
- *remain focused on the child and their needs and development;*
- *be evidence-based, including analysis of the evidence.*

The need to work collaboratively is emphasised, ensuring that the views and feelings of applicants are heard. One of the tools in Form C allows prospective carers to provide information in their own words. As Adams (2017) states:

> *It can be hugely helpful for fostering panel members and others if they can see the actual words of the applicant(s) as part of the paperwork submitted.*

Immediate placement

It is possible for a local authority to place a child, whom they are looking after and who requires an immediate placement, with a connected person. Temporary approval as a foster carer may be given under Regulation 24 of the Care Planning, Placement and Case Review (England) Regulations 2010 for up to 16 weeks. Regulation 25 allows for an extension of up to a further eight weeks if the full assessment requires this time for completion but requires that the views of the fostering panel are sought. If a full assessment is completed but a qualifying determination is made that the carer is not suitable and the carer applies for an independent review by the IRM, their temporary approval may be extended until the review is completed and a final decision made. No further extension of approval is possible in either situation. Guidance 5.57 makes clear that there is no right to review by the IRM of a person who is temporarily approved under the 2010 Regulations if the fostering service decides not to undertake a full assessment under the 2011 fostering regulations.

Family and Friends Guidance 5.8 makes clear that:

> *These provisions relating to temporary approval are intended to be used exceptionally and in circumstances which could not easily have been foreseen, when it is not possible to undertake a full foster care assessment prior to placement.*

However, given court timescales, this is often the standard route by which many family and friends placements are made.

Family and Friends Guidance 5.12 states: 'Authorities will need to nominate an officer with authority to grant temporary approval of foster carers under Regulation 24'. It suggests that this will usually be the fostering service decision-maker.

The matters to be taken into account when assessing the suitability of a connected person on a temporary basis are in Regulation 24(2) and Schedule 4 of the Care Planning, Placement and Case Review (England) Regulations 2010 and in Family and Friends Guidance 5.8–5.11.

These are minimum requirements. The quality of any existing relationship between the child and the proposed carer must be assessed. The home must be visited to ensure its suitability for the child. The child's wishes and feelings must be ascertained subject to the child's age and understanding. The views of the child's parents and others with parental responsibility must also be ascertained.

Issues concerning family and friends as foster carers

As previously stated, there are some clear advantages for children who are living with family and friends. However, strengths such as an established relationship and a sense of family belonging must be weighed up against any limitations. Panels need to be aware that sometimes different expectations may apply to family and friends foster carers than those applied to unrelated foster carers. These can include more flexibility regarding accommodation arrangements, for example, sharing a bedroom with another child in the household, as well as a number of other issues (see below). The crucial issue is making an appropriate placement for a particular child.

National Minimum Standards

There may be concerns expressed that the prospective family and friends foster carers do not meet the NMS. It is important to note that these are standards for the fostering service, and the agency and panel will need to consider whether prospective carers can be supported to attain the standard/s required. For family and friends foster carers, case law sets out that the first consideration is 'whether it is in the welfare interests of the children to be placed with these carers' (quoted in *Knowsley MBC v X & Ors* 2018] EWFC 42).

Age and health

It may be appropriate for a local authority to approve a much older (or much younger) relative or friend as a foster carer for a specific child. There may also be health concerns regarding the carer. Such flexibility may not be given in the case of someone applying to be a foster carer for any child. It is the significance of the relationship and the fact that the relative or friend is able to meet the specific child's needs that will be the primary consideration. It will be important that contingency plans are fully explored. Family and Friends Guidance 5.35 addresses this and notes that 'specialist advice may be needed, such as from the fostering service's medical adviser'.

Convictions

As noted in Chapter 4, people cannot be approved as foster carers if they have committed certain offences specified by Regulation 26. However, this does not apply to relatives or friends who wish to foster a particular child (see Regulation 26(8)). A relative or friend of the child may have a number of past convictions. The implications of these for their ability to care for a specific child will of course need to be analysed and given appropriate weight. Family and Friends Guidance 5.38 covers the possibility of approving a connected person who may have a conviction that would otherwise debar them from fostering.

> *Such a decision should only be made when the decision-maker is satisfied that approving*

the applicant is the most appropriate way to safeguard and promote the child's welfare.

Smoking

As noted in Chapter 2, Practice Note 68 (CoramBAAF, 2018a) advises that children under the age of five or those who have disabilities or respiratory difficulties should not be placed with carers who smoke. Usually, applicants would not be approved to care for children in such cases. For relatives and friends, the health risk posed to the child should be fully explored and given weight against the potential benefit of being placed with a family member or friend. Smoking cessation, where possible, should be encouraged and supported. E-cigarettes have become more popular. They may have benefits for people trying to quit smoking and the risk to children from passive smoke is lower. However, there may be risks of unhelpful role modelling and a possible "re-normalising" of smoking in some cases. Liquid nicotine is also highly toxic. This again would need consideration. (See Gould (2015) in *Promoting the Health of Children in Public Care*.)

Child protection

All foster carers are expected to keep children safe and protected in their care. These same standards should apply to family and friends, whether or not they are being approved as foster carers. The panel will need to have evidence of the family member or friend's ability to keep the child safe, including protecting the child from any risk posed by the birth parent(s), as appropriate. Family and Friends Guidance 5.22–5.25 recognises that:

> *In some families the tensions and difficulties that arise between family members may outweigh the benefits of making a placement within the family networks.*

It will be necessary to know that the family member or friend is working openly and honestly with the local authority, and vice versa. It will be important to evaluate whether the family member or friend is not or is no longer part of the difficulties that led to the child being looked after. This needs to be considered carefully and fairly, without prejudice.

Family members who may be approved as foster carers for their relative's child may have very strong emotions about what has happened. For example, grandparents caring for a grandchild will have their own feelings regarding their son or daughter who might have hurt the child. Relatives may feel angry and guilty about what has occurred in their family. There can be anger towards local authority involvement and a lack of understanding of procedures and practice. This requires sensitivity, openness and understanding on the part of the local authority.

Views of the child

NMS 30.3 requires that:

> *In deciding whether a relative, friend or other connected person should be approved as a foster carer, the decision-maker takes into account the needs, wishes and feelings of the child and the capacity of the carer to meet these.*

As Family and Friends Guidance 5.16 notes, this clarifies that 'there is no need to consider their suitability to care for other children, just for the specific child to whom they are connected'. Some placements may involve a change of area and Family and Friends Guidance 5.25 states that 'It is important to discuss the priorities of placement with the child concerned and to take account of their wishes and feelings'.

NMS 30.5 further states:

> *When assessing an individual's capacity to be a family and friends foster carer, the likely length of the placement, the age of the child, the wishes and feelings or any concerns of the child and if appropriate, the capacity of the wider family to contribute to the child's long-term care, are taken into account.*

Panel members will need to be aware of their own values and attitudes about family members and friends when weighing up whether or not they should be approved as foster carers for a specific child. Judgements about people's ability to care for specific children need to be based on the evidence presented in the assessment report of the family member or friend, and in the report provided regarding the child. Panels will need to consider the strengths of a placement with a relative or friend, but also need to be clear about where there are vulnerabilities. The support and training needs of the family member or friend as a foster carer should be fully explored. In all matters, it is always the child's welfare that must be the primary consideration, and the assessment report needs to set out clearly how the carer will meet the needs of the looked after child. The fact that they are a relative is not in itself a reason for approval. On occasion, panels will not recommend the approval or the continued approval of an existing placement. As with any recommendation, the panel will need to be clear as to its reasons for that recommendation.

Report to panel

Family and Friends Guidance 5.19 states:

> *A different approach may be needed to assessing family and friends foster carers compared to other foster carer applications. The format used by a local authority for presenting assessment reports to the fostering panel may not be appropriate for family and friends assessments if it does not allow for a focus on how the carers will meet the specific needs of the child concerned.*

Local authorities are currently using a variety of formats to try to convey this information in a clear and helpful way to panels.

As previously stated, CoramBAAF's Form C – Connected Persons (Family and Friends) Report England can be used in the assessment of connected persons at various different stages of placement including temporary approval assessments and for assessments of prospective foster carers and special guardians.

Where approval is recommended, the panel will need to be clear as to the terms of that approval, and whether they are being approved as short-term or long-term carers for the specific child. Should long-term approval be sought, it may be necessary for the plan to be referred to a panel that considers permanence plans.

If a child moves from the care of the family member or friend, the approval of the family member or friend as a foster carer will need to be terminated by the fostering service provider.

6 Reviews and changes and terminations of approval

Legal functions

The legal functions of a fostering panel also include the following under Regulation 25(1) of the Regulations:

(c) to recommend whether or not a person remains suitable to be a foster parent, and whether or not the terms of their approval (if any) remain appropriate –

  (i) on the first review carried out in accordance with Regulation 28(2); and

  (ii) on the occasion of any other review, if requested to do so by the fostering service provider in accordance with Regulation 28(5); and

(d) to consider any case referred to it under Regulation… 28(10).

The cases referred to in Regulation 28(10) are those where the foster carer has made written representations because the fostering service provider has notified them that they propose to terminate or to alter the terms of the foster carer's approval.

The fostering panel must also:

(a) advise, where appropriate, on the procedures under which reviews in accordance with Regulation 28 are carried out by the fostering service provider, and periodically monitor their effectiveness (Regulation 25(4)).

Regulation 28 sets out the procedure to be followed for reviews, changes to terms of approval, and terminations.

Reviews of foster carers

The approval of foster carers is required to be reviewed at least annually. Undertaking such reviews involves sensitivity, careful analysis and rigour as they are critical in building and improving quality foster care for children (see Adams, 2014 and Cosis Brown, 2015). They involve establishing whether or not a foster carer and their household remain suitable to care for foster children and that their terms of approval remain appropriate, should be changed or even terminated.

As NMS 13.8 sets out:

Reviews of foster carers' approval are sufficiently thorough to allow the fostering service to properly satisfy itself about their carers' ongoing suitability to foster.

Agencies will have developed a range of ways of conducting reviews of foster carers, but they will need to include the following: an appraisal of the carer's abilities and experience over the year; the numbers and types of placements and any issues arising; the views of foster children, subject to age and understanding; and the views of the foster carer and any views of responsible authorities that have placed children within the preceding year (see Regulation 28(3)(a) and (b)).

Training, Support and Development Standards

It should be noted that within their first year of approval, foster carers are expected to complete the Training, Support and Development Standards for foster carers (TSDS) (Department for Education, 2012). For the first annual review and at subsequent reviews, it can therefore be helpful to refer to how the carer has met or continues to meet the Standards. They include: an awareness of key principles and values essential for fostering children and young people; the foster carer role itself; the ability to promote healthy care for children and young people; the ability to communicate effectively; having a good understanding of children and young people's development; having an understanding of the importance of keeping children and young people safe from harm; and being willing to develop oneself through learning, reflection and training. There are separate Standards for family and friends foster carers (which they should complete within 18 months). There are also separate Standards for short break foster carers (Department for Education, 2012, and Appendix 2).

Review report and review meeting

A written report should be undertaken by the foster carers' supervising social worker and should include the feedback and views as required by Regulation 28(3). Additional information should include the views of any children of the foster carers and the views of birth parents, if possible. The views of third parties, for example, the IRO for the child, and staff at the fostered child's school or nursery, can also be very valuable. Useful reference can be made to the National Minimum Standards, the Training, Support and Development Standards and the Secure Base Model in assessing fostering skills and knowledge. If the foster carers are fostering as a couple, both carers should be interviewed and appraised as part of the review. Although not a statutory requirement, many agencies arrange for foster carers' health reviews and DBS checks to be repeated every two or three years.

If not a first annual review, it is important to establish whether previously identified strengths remain from the previous review and whether any areas for development have been addressed. Significant issues from supervision sessions or from unannounced visits should be highlighted. Training needs and areas for development should be fully explored. Any complaints, allegations or concerns should be addressed. The report should conclude by setting out whether the person(s) continue to be suitable to foster and whether the terms of approval continue to be appropriate (See Cosis Brown, 2015, p84 for detailed information on reports, and for a Foster Carer Review Form and guide, see Adams, 2014).

Following the completion of the supervising social worker's report, a review meeting is usually held. It is good practice if this is chaired by a manager independent of the fostering team, i.e. a team manager of another team or by an independent fostering reviewing officer. The foster carers and supervising social worker will attend. The meeting allows an opportunity for full discussion of the carers' experience of fostering, recognition of their work and agreement on any action plan, as required. The reviewing officer will also write a report and recommend whether the person(s) continues to be suitable to foster and whether the terms of approval continue to be appropriate.

Reviews – the role of the panel

The fostering panel is required to consider the first review of all foster carers and make a recommendation regarding their continued suitability. This must take place within one year of approval. Panels must also consider reviews where a change to the terms of approval of the foster carer is proposed and there is no agreement to the proposed change by the carer. In addition, the panel may consider subsequent reviews if referred by the fostering service provider. It is also required to advise on procedures about how reviews are carried out and to monitor these. Information on reviews should therefore be provided to the panel by the fostering service and opportunity given for discussion on a regular basis.

There should be clear procedures for when to refer reviews (other than the first one) to the panel. Good practice would suggest the following should be referred:

- For first reviews, panels could consider reviews of new carers at six months and then at one year.
- All reviews where significant changes of approval are required, even where the foster carer agrees with the changes.
- Reviews following significant events affecting the carer(s).
- Reviews following child protection concerns or allegations made about standards of care provided by foster carers.
- Reviews could be referred every three years, even where there is no change, in order to provide some external monitoring and scrutiny of agency and fostering practice.

In order to consider a foster carer's review, the panel should receive the review paperwork as discussed earlier. This should include the terms of the foster carer's approval and any recommendations for changing that approval. Again, alongside their supervising social worker, the foster carer should be invited to attend the panel to discuss their review and their fostering experience over the past year. It may be necessary to invite them to participate via telephone or video conferencing. The foster carer should have contributed to their review and seen a copy of the reports provided to the panel. The review of the carer's skills and abilities should be the primary focus. However, the panel may on occasion raise questions about plans for children if there are significant concerns about drift, delay and the appropriateness of particular placements. The panel will then proceed to make a recommendation regarding the carer's continued suitability to foster.

If, following a review and taking into account any recommendation of the panel, the fostering service provider decides that the foster carer and their household continue to be suitable and that the terms of approval continue to be appropriate, the decision-maker must confirm this decision in writing (see CoramBAAF, 2019, and Appendix 3).

Deferring a review

As in considering approvals covered in Chapter 4, the panel may occasionally defer making a recommendation when considering a review. This is only appropriate in cases where the review is of poor quality or significant issues have not been properly addressed so that it is not possible for the panel to make a fair or informed recommendation. The panel should therefore specify what is needed and in what timescale. The panel will need to make a careful judgement, taking into account any advice provided by the fostering service provider. If the review is deferred, no recommendation has been made by the panel and the foster carer continues to be approved.

Change of approval

In order to change a foster carer's terms of approval, a review of the foster carer's approval should be undertaken, as set out earlier. The fostering service decision-maker can then issue a qualifying determination (see below) setting out the proposed change, with or without a recommendation from the panel. The decision to change the terms of approval can then be implemented at the end of 28 days from the date of the qualifying determination. As previously stated, it is good practice to refer such reviews to the panel as changes to terms of approval are often significant.

The Regulations as amended set out that in cases where the *only* change is to the terms of approval, and this needs to be achieved quickly for good reason, a determination of the proposed change can be made by the fostering service provider in agreement with the foster carer. The fostering service provider must set out the proposed change in writing and include whether there are likely to be any additional support needs for the foster carer or members of their household (including any foster children) and if so, how they will be met. It must also ask the foster carer for their written agreement to the proposed change to their approval. If the foster carer agrees to the change, it is then possible to waive the 28-day waiting period and implement the decision immediately, in which case the decision is not a qualifying determination. This written agreement must be given freely by the foster carer. If the foster carer does not agree to the change to their terms of approval, the decision cannot be implemented until 28 days from the date of the qualifying determination. The foster carer can make representations to the fostering service or to the IRM within the 28-day period (see Pippa Bow and Paul Adams, October 2017, https://corambaaf.org.uk/updates/usual-fostering-limit-exemptions-and-terms-approval-foster-carers-england.).

Qualifying determination, representation and IRM process

As stated above, if the foster carer does not agree with a proposed change to their terms of approval, it is defined as a qualifying determination. They may, within 28 days, either submit written representations to the fostering service decision-maker, or apply for a review of the determination to the IRM. However, it should be noted that Regulation 28(8) clarifies that there is no right to apply to the IRM where the fostering service provider is no longer satisfied that Regulation 26(8) applies, i.e. that the welfare of the child requires that placement, despite the carer or a member of their household having a caution or conviction for a specified offence.

If representations are received by the decision-maker, the matter must be referred to the fostering panel before a final decision is made taking into account the fostering panel's recommendation. If the matter is referred to the IRM, the decision-maker must take account of its recommendation, as well as that of the original fostering panel (if a panel was involved), before reaching a decision.

The agency must then give the foster carer written notice of the revised terms of approval.

Regard must also be given to Regulation 28(14), which states that:

> A copy of any notice given under this regulation must be sent to the placing authority for any child placed with the foster parent (unless the placing authority is also the fostering service provider) and the area authority for any child placed with the foster parent.

Emergency placement outside agreed terms of approval

Regulation 23(1) of the Care Planning, Placement and Case Review (England) Regulations 2010 requires that any emergency placement outside a foster carer's terms of approval 'is for no longer than six working days'. When the period of six working days expires, the placement must be terminated unless the foster carer's terms of approval have been amended so that they are consistent with the placement. The Care Planning, Placement and Case Review Guidance 3.92 makes clear that these placements should be made 'exceptionally in unforeseen circumstances...' and that 'Research evidence consistently shows that placements outside the terms of approval are significantly more likely to result in placement breakdown...'

Many agencies approve foster carers with wider terms of approval, allowing flexibility in placements that can be made. As stated in Chapter 4, evidence should be provided of the capacity of the carers to meet the needs of children in such a range.

Terminations of approval

The approvals of foster carers end in a number of different ways. Most approvals end when foster carers themselves decide to resign from fostering. This may be due to retirement after a number of years, or a change of career, or a change in circumstances. It may be that the foster carer wishes to have a break from fostering for a period of time. It may be that a foster carer wishes to be approved by another fostering service provider. In all such cases foster carers are required to give notice in writing to the fostering service provider and their approval is terminated with effect from 28 days from the date on which the agency receives this notice (Regulation 28(13)).

Resignation – no child in placement

Guidance 5.59 states that:

> The decision-maker does not have the power to decline a resignation...but this need not prevent the fostering service from forming a view about the person's future suitability to be a foster carer. Once a foster carer has resigned, the fostering service has no responsibility to confirm resignation through panel, although it may be helpful to notify the panel to inform its monitoring role.

This could be a paper exercise with a brief report and a copy of the foster carer's letter of resignation. This should enable panel members to be aware of any agency or foster carer practice issues that have led to a resignation.

Resignation – child in placement

If there is a child in placement and the carer wishes to move to another fostering service, the situation is more complex. The Fostering Network has drawn up a Protocol concerning the movement of carers between agencies. This stipulates that each fostering service will include in their contract with foster carers a clause that makes it clear that no carer may join another fostering service provider whilst they have a child in placement, unless arrangements for the continuing care of the child are made to the satisfaction of the placing authority and the existing fostering service.

Resignation – following concerns

There are occasions where significant concerns, allegations or complaints have been made against a foster carer and the agency wishes to terminate their approval through the panel recommendation and decision-maker process. However, the foster carers have tendered their resignation and this will automatically end their approval in 28 days. In these circumstances, the agency will often wish to refer the full matter to the fostering panel. Many agencies ask their panels to note the resignation and to consider whether they would have given serious consideration to recommending termination of approval. The foster carers should be invited to the panel at which their case is considered, and asked to explain and defend the concerns, allegations or complaints about their practice. The panel's views and those of the agency are then held on the foster carer's file and can be provided in references to other agencies if necessary. The foster carers will be able to challenge any findings placed on their file through the fostering service provider's complaints procedure.

Terminations of approval in other circumstances

Occasionally it will be necessary for fostering service providers to terminate a foster carer's approval due to significant changes in their circumstances or due to concerns about poor, or in some cases, abusive care. In some cases, this may be because there has been inadequate agency support and/or placements made of children outside of a foster carer's approval range. There are other situations where foster carers or members of their household have deliberately harmed and abused children. It is essential that a fair process is in place to deal with such actions as the consequences for foster families can be far-reaching.

If, therefore, following a review, a fostering service provider proposes to terminate a foster carer's approval, it must notify the carer in writing, with the decision-maker's reasons and a copy of the panel recommendation, if the panel was involved. This is again a qualifying determination. The procedure then mirrors that for changes of approval and the qualifying determination, representation and IRM process apply (see earlier in this chapter). Written notice of the final decision must be given under Regulation 28(12)(a) or (b) and regard must be given to the need to give copies of notices to placing and area authorities.

Terminations: the role of the panel

There is no absolute requirement to refer all terminations of approval cases to panel for a recommendation. The fostering service provider is required to take account of any recommendation made by the fostering panel if the matter is referred to the panel. It would, however, be good practice to routinely refer significant cases and this should be clarified in internal procedures regarding reviews. At the very least, the panel should be informed of these as part of its monitoring function. Although not stipulated in the Regulations, best practice would suggest that terminations of approval should be referred to the panel using the following process.

This process would require the following:

- completion of full review paperwork, including details of complaints, allegations and concerns;
- a clear account of the process of the investigation, including provision of independent support to the foster carers;
- an explanation of any mitigating factors;
- a full account of the agency's work with the carers, including support, supervision and development opportunities;
- recommendations as to change of approval or termination of approval set out and clear evidence provided as to the reasons.

The foster carer(s) should have read this report and should have been invited to provide their own observations in writing for the panel to consider.

As for all matters, the process for attending the panel needs to be fair and transparent. It is suggested, therefore, that the following process could be applied.

- The panel prepares its questions prior to attendance of workers and carers.
- The foster carer(s) and their support person (if wished for), the supervising social worker, the independent reviewing officer (if applicable) and a manager (if necessary) are invited to attend the panel for questions and observations.
- They are each asked questions in turn.
- They are all then asked to leave the panel.
- The panel then proceeds to deliberate and reach its recommendation. The panel should always reserve the right to invite any of the parties back into the panel meeting for further clarification of points raised. Exceptionally, the panel may wish to hear from any party separately.

The Chair and the agency adviser should inform the parties verbally of the panel's recommendation once reached and its reasons. The panel's recommendation would then be referred to the fostering service provider for a decision or qualifying determination to be made and the representation and IRM process would apply.

If a carer brings a supporter to panel, this could be a solicitor but it would need to be made clear that a solicitor was present as a supporter not as a legal representative. It should be the panel, through the Chair, that decides whether or not the supporter is able to speak in panel. Should a supporter attend, it will be important to ensure compliance with the GDPR and DPA 2018, particularly in relation to the personal data of any children who have been placed with the foster carer (see Adams and Jordan, 2019).

These cases are complex and stressful. It can be helpful for the panel to take a break during the process and to have some time to debrief afterwards. Difficult dynamics may be evident between the agency and the carers and there may be some strong and painful feelings. These need to be understood by the panel and feedback provided to the agency regarding practice concerns, if necessary.

As stated, there are occasions where the approval of a foster carer has been terminated for reasons of misconduct. This could include suspected or proven abuse of a child. In these situations, the fostering service provider needs to consider whether the foster carer's name should be referred to the Disclosure and Barring Service. In such cases, the panel may be asked to form a view regarding this when making its recommendation regarding termination of approval.

Similarly, Ofsted requires that serious complaints against carers are notified to them. There is no definition of "serious" but it is likely that such occurrences would warrant a review of the carers' approval. Again, the panel should be involved to consider the review and to recommend any changes in approval and whether the complaint should be referred to Ofsted.

7 Monitoring and quality assurance

Monitoring

The panel is legally required to 'oversee the conduct of assessments' and 'to give advice and make recommendations on such other matters or cases as the fostering service provider may refer to it' under Regulation 25(4). Furthermore, the NMS 14.2 requires that:

> Panels provide a quality assurance feedback to the fostering service provider on the quality of reports being presented to the panel.

The panel needs therefore to monitor the quality of reports and work undertaken by the fostering service provider. Inadequate or poor reports should be challenged and recommendations deferred, if necessary, for better quality information and assessments to be provided. Many agencies provide a quality of report feedback sheet on all assessments and review reports presented to panel. This is completed by the panel Chair or vice-chair and should incorporate the views of panel members at the meeting (see Appendix 7). Feedback usually covers the strengths of the assessment report, any concerns, any learning points for practice and sometimes includes a rating as to whether the report is viewed as outstanding, very good, good, adequate or inadequate.

The speed of assessments should also be monitored so that carers are not waiting unduly for their applications to be approved. NMS 14.4 states that the fostering panel should make its recommendation on the suitability of a prospective foster carer within eight months of the receipt of the prospective foster carer's application to be assessed.

Panels should be aware of the preparation, training and support provided by the agency. It would be useful to set up forums where there can be exchanges of views between panels and social workers. Regular and consistent feedback from foster carers about the assessment process should be obtained.

Good practice suggests that panels receive management information on the outcome of foster carer reviews. It is also important to monitor the range of foster carers available in relation to the profile of children needing foster carers.

As previously noted in Chapter 4, the usual fostering limit for a foster carer is to care for three children, unless they are all part of the same sibling group. Sometimes it will be necessary for local authorities to grant an exemption from the fostering limit in particular cases so that more children can be placed. These children must be named and only the area authority in which the foster family live can grant the exemption. (See paragraph 4 of Schedule 7 to the Children Act 1989.) The terms of the carer's approval also need to allow it. It can be helpful to inform the fostering panel at its next meeting so that it can monitor any exemptions made. The panel should raise concerns with the fostering service provider if it considers that the exemption should not continue. It is essential that the panel and the fostering service provider are fully satisfied that such arrangements are working in the best interests of children and within the capabilities of the foster carers.

The panel needs information on all of these issues in order to monitor, to ask questions and to assist the agency in developing recruitment strategies and support packages for foster carers as required. It should know about the development of working relationships with other fostering service providers as necessary.

Annual report

Good practice suggests that an annual report should be prepared detailing the work of the fostering service, including the numbers and profiles of foster carers and children; the number of disruptions; recruitment and retention strategies; training and support; strengths and achievements of the service; quality of reports; performance targets; the work of the panel; and future areas for development. This report should be approved by the fostering service provider and the Chair and made available to panel members, foster carers, children and young people in foster care, elected members, responsible individuals as well as to the managers and staff within the agency.

Business meetings

Panel meetings are often busy with a number of items to consider. It is important, however, to allow time occasionally for business issues to be discussed. Specific quarterly meetings or the first half hour of a panel meeting could be devoted to business items. These may include agreeing areas of concern to be fed back to the agency or discussing specific panel matters such as the need to fill a particular vacancy, or agreeing/reviewing the format the minutes should take. It can be helpful to involve the decision-maker in at least some of these.

Training

It is essential that central list/panel members have opportunities for training. NMS 23.10 states:

> *Each person on the central list is given the opportunity of attending an annual joint training day with the fostering service's fostering staff.*

And NMS 23.11:

> *Each person on the central list has access to appropriate training and skills development and is kept abreast of relevant changes to legislation and guidance.*

Panel members should have the opportunity to reflect on the role and function of the panel, any issues arising, and new developments in fostering. Members should have the opportunity to reflect on anti-discriminatory practice and to look at how their personal attitudes and values impinge on the panel process. Training days can offer time and space for panel members to get to know each other and aid in the development of effective group working.

Conclusion

Children's welfare is paramount

The children looked after in foster care are often vulnerable or challenging, but also rewarding! They have a right to safe and protective environments where their needs can be met. Skilled and committed foster carers can and do provide this for many thousands of children every day.

It is essential that fostering panels are fully equipped to undertake their key role in facilitating and monitoring the care provided by foster carers and by fostering service providers. Panel members may build up a close and supportive relationship with workers in their fostering agency. However, they also need to retain some independence and must not be afraid to question and to comment on gaps or failings as well as praising good practice in the service. In turn, the fostering service provider must take account of their views. It must always be kept in mind that the service is there to meet the needs of children and that their welfare is paramount at all times.

References

References

Adams P (2014) *Undertaking a Foster Carer Review*, London: BAAF

Adams P (2015) *Dogs and Pets in Fostering and Adoption*, London: BAAF

Adams P (2017) *Undertaking Checks and References in Fostering and Adoption Assessments*, London: CoramBAAF

Adams P and Jordan L (2019) *Complying with the GDPR and DPA 2018: A good practice guide for fostering services in England*, London: CoramBAAF

Aldred K and Rodwell H (2018) *Supporting the Mental Health of Looked After and Adopted Children*, London: CoramBAAF

BAAF (2014) *Paperless Fostering and Adoption Panels*, Practice Note 56, London: BAAF

BAAF (2015) *Using the Internet in Adoption and Fostering Assessments*, Practice Note 55, London: BAAF

Borthwick S and Donnelly S (2013) *Concurrent Planning: Achieving early permanence for babies and young children*, London: BAAF

Broad B and Skinner A (2005) *Relative Benefits: Placing children in kinship care*, London: BAAF

Chapman R (2014) *Undertaking a Fostering Assessment* (2nd edn), London: BAAF

Cocker C and Brown HC (2010) 'Sex, sexuality and relationships: developing confidence and discernment when assessing lesbian and gay prospective adopters', *Adoption & Fostering*, 34:1, pp 20–32

CoramBAAF (2017) *Decisions about the Assessments of Couples and Other Partnerships in Foster Care (England)*, Practice Note 65, London: CoramBAAF

CoramBAAF (2018a) *Reducing the Risks of Environmental Tobacco Smoke for Looked After Children and their Carers*, Practice Note 68, London: CoramBAAF

CoramBAAF (2018b) *Assessing and Supporting Transgender Foster Carers and Adopters*, Practice Note 69, London: CoramBAAF

CoramBAAF (2019) *The Fostering Decision-Maker (England)*, Practice Note 70, London: CoramBAAF

Conroy Harris A (2019) *Child Care Law: A summary of the law in England*, London: CoramBAAF

Cosis Brown H (2015) *Foster Carer Reviews: Process, practicalities and best practice* (3rd edn), London: BAAF

Department for Education (2011) *Family and Friends Care: Statutory guidance for local authorities*, London: DfE

Department for Education (2012) *Training, Support and Development Standards for Foster Carers*, London, DfE

Department for Education (2018) *Children Looked After by Local Authorities, Year Ending 31 March 2018*, London: DfE

Department for Education (2018) *Fostering Better Outcomes: The Government response to the Education Select Committee report into fostering and foster care in England*, London: DfE

Department of Health (2012) *Alcohol Advice*, London: DH

Dibben E and Howorth V (2016) *Adoption by Foster Carers: A guide to preparing, assessing and supporting foster carers adopting children in their care*, London: CoramBAAF

Dibben E and Howorth V (2017) *The Role of Fostering for Adoption in Achieving Early Permanence for Children*, London: CoramBAAF

Farmer E and Moyers S (2008) *Kinship Care: Fostering effective family and friends placements*, London: Jessica Kingsley Publishers

Fursland E (2011) *Foster Care and Social Networking*, London: BAAF

Gould J (2015) 'Adult health assessment', in Merredew F and Sampeys C (eds) *Promoting the Health of Children in Public Care*, London: BAAF, pp 247–271

Griffin B (2016) *Croydon Safeguarding Children Board Serious Case Review: 'Claire'*, available at: http://croydonlcsb.org.uk/wp-content/uploads/2017/01/CSCB-SCR-Claire-Overview-Report.pdf

House of Commons Education Committee (2017) *Fostering: First report of session 2017–19*, London: House of Commons

Hunt J, Waterhouse S and Lutman E (2008) *Keeping them in the Family: Outcomes for children placed in kinship care through care proceedings*, London: BAAF

IRM (2018) *Annual Report*, available at: www.gov.uk/government/organisations/independent-review-mechanism

De Jong A and Donnelly S (2015) *Recruiting, Assessing and Supporting Lesbian and Gay Adopters*, London: BAAF

Lawson K and Cann R (2019) *State of the Nation's Foster Care*, London: Fostering Network

Lord J and Cullen D (2016) *Effective Adoption Panels*, London: CoramBAAF

Mather M and Lehner K (2010) *Evaluating Obesity in Substitute Carers*, London: BAAF

Merredew F and Sampeys C (eds) (2015) *Promoting the Health of Children in Public Care*, London: BAAF

Merredew F and Sampeys C (2017) *Undertaking a Health Assessment*, London: CoramBAAF

Mervyn-Smith O (2018) *Kinship Care: State of the Nation 2018*, London: Grandparents Plus

Narey M and Owers M (2018) *Foster Care in England: A review for the Department for Education*, London: DfE

NICE (2018) *Stop Smoking Interventions and Services*, Guideline 92, London: NICE

Pratt J (2019) *A Guide to Writing Panel Minutes*, London: BAAF

Schofield G and Beek M (2014) *The Secure Base Model: Promoting attachment and resilience in foster care and adoption*, London: BAAF

Sellick C, Thoburn J and Philpot T (2004) *What Works in Adoption and Foster Care?*, London: Barnardo's

Simmonds J (2011) *The Role of Special Guardianship*, London: BAAF

Sinclair I (2005) *Fostering Now: Messages from research*, London: Jessica Kingsley Publishers

Smith F and Brann C (2016) *Fostering Now*, London: BAAF

World Health Organization (1999) *World Health Report 1999*, Geneva: WHO

Acts, Regulations, Standards and Guidance

Acts

Children Act 1989

Data Protection Act 2018

Protection of Children Act 1999

Adoption and Children Act 2002

Children Act 2004

Children and Families Act 2014

Children and Social Work Act 2017

Regulations

Children (Private Arrangements for Fostering) Regulations 2005

Adoption Agencies Regulations 2005

Special Guardianship Regulations 2005

Care Planning, Placement and Case Review (England) Regulations 2010

Fostering Services (England) Regulations 2011

Care Planning, Placement and Case Review and Fostering Services (Miscellaneous Amendments) Regulations 2013

Adoption and Care Planning (Miscellaneous Amendments) Regulations 2014

Care Planning and Fostering (Miscellaneous Amendments) (England) Regulations 2015

General Data Protection Regulation 2018

Standards

Fostering Services: National Minimum Standards 2011

Training, Support and Development Standards for Foster Care, 2012

Guidance

Children Act 1989 Guidance Volume 4: Fostering Services 2011 (as amended)

Family and Friends Care: Statutory Guidance for Local Authorities 2011

Assessment and Approval of Foster Care: Amendments to the Children Act 1989 Guidance and Regulations, Fostering Services, 2013

Children Act 1989 Guidance Volume 2: Care Planning, Placement and Case Review 2015

Glossary

Accommodated

Under section 20 of the Children Act 1989, the local authority is required to "provide accommodation" for children "in need" in certain circumstances.

The local authority does not acquire parental responsibility merely by accommodating a child and the arrangements for the child must normally be agreed with the parent(s) who, subject to certain circumstances, are entitled to remove the children from local authority accommodation at any time.

Adoption

The complete and irrevocable transfer, by court order, of all parental rights and responsibilities for a child or young person under the age of 18 to a new parent or parents.

Adoption panel

Adoption agencies (local authorities, regional adoption agencies (RAAs) and voluntary adoption agencies (VAAs)) are required to set up an adoption panel which must consider and make recommendations on children for whom adoption is the plan and there is no court involvement, on prospective adopters and on matches between prospective adopters and children. The organisation and general functioning of an adoption panel are very similar to that of a fostering panel.

Adoption and fostering panel

Some local authorities and VAAs have panels which, in addition to the adoption considerations described above, also consider and make recommendations in relation to fostering matters.

Agencies

In this guide, this refers to local authority and independent fostering services.

Area authority

The local authority in whose area the child and foster carers are living, where that authority is not the responsible authority.

CAFCASS

The Children and Family Court Advisory and Support Service is a national non-departmental public body for England. It has brought together the services provided by the Family Court Welfare Service, the Guardian ad Litem Services and the Children's Division of the Official Solicitor. CAFCASS is independent of the courts, social services, education and health authorities and all similar agencies.

Care order

Applies only to England and Wales. A child who is subject to a care order is described as being "in care". A care order gives the local authority parental responsibility for the child but does not deprive the parent(s) of this. Nevertheless, the local authority may limit the extent to which parents may exercise their parental responsibility and may override parental wishes in the interests of the child's welfare.

Care plan

An agreed plan for looking after a child and meeting that child's current and future needs, made by the placing authority under the Children Act 1989.

Care proceedings

The court process involved in consideration of whether or not to make a care order.

Central list

Fostering service providers must set up a central list of people, who must be checked, inducted and trained, and from which the members of each panel must be chosen. Adoption agencies must do the same thing in relation to adoption panels.

Child arrangements order

An order under the Children Act 1989 (as amended by the Children and Families Act 2014) settling the arrangements as to when and with whom the child is to live, spend time or otherwise have contact. Where a child arrangements order settles that a child should live with a person who does not already have parental responsibility for the child (e.g. a relative or foster carer), that person will acquire parental responsibility subject to certain restrictions (e.g. they will not be able to consent to the child's adoption). If the child arrangements order is for contact, the court has discretion as to whether to grant parental responsibility. Parental responsibility, given in connection with a child arrangements order, will only last as long as the order. An exception is where the child arrangements order is made in favour of a parent without parental responsibility (unmarried father or second female parent), in which case the court must consider whether the parent should have parental responsibility and, if so, must also make a separate order for parental responsibility under section 4 or section 4ZA, which will not be dependent on the continuation of the child arrangements order. A child arrangements order can last until the child's 18th birthday.

Child arrangements order allowance

Local authorities have a power to contribute to the cost of a child's maintenance when the child is living with somebody under a child arrangements order (Children Act 1989, schedule 1, para 15), provided that they are not living with a parent or step- parent. A financial contribution under this power is normally referred to as a child arrangements order allowance, and each authority will have its own policy about how it will exercise its discretion on applications for payment of an allowance.

Child's review

Regulations prescribe that looked after children must have their care and the plans for them regularly reviewed. Reviews must happen, as a minimum, a month after the child starts being looked after, three months later, then every six months.

Children's guardian

A person appointed by the court to safeguard a child's interests in court proceedings (formerly called a guardian ad litem). Their duties include presenting a report to the court.

Concurrent planning

This is the term given to a scheme in which children, usually babies or toddlers, for whom there is a chance that they might return home to their birth family, are placed with families who will foster them with this aim. However, the foster carers are also approved as adopters and will adopt the child, should the planned return home not be successful. In this way, the moves that a child may otherwise have to make are minimised. These schemes have to be run with the agreement and co-operation of the local court and to tight timescales.

Connected person

A relative, friend or other person connected with a looked after child. A person in the last category may be someone who knows the child in a more professional capacity, such as a teacher.

Contact/contact order

Contact may be used to mean visits, including residential visits or other forms of direct face-to-face contact between a child and another individual, or it may mean indirect ways of keeping in touch (e.g. letters, social media or telephone calls including letters sent via a third party). Orders setting out contact arrangements under s.8 of the Children Act 1989 are known as "child arrangements orders". An order for contact to a child in care may be made under s.34 of the Children Act 1989 and requires the local authority looking after the child to allow contact between the child and a person named in the order. An order under s.34(4) of the Children Act 1989 allows the local authority to refuse contact between the child and a named person who would otherwise be entitled to reasonable contact. A contact order under the Children Act 1989 can now only be made in public proceedings.

Decision-maker

A senior person within the fostering service or a trustee or director of the fostering service, who is a social worker with at least three years' post-qualifying experience in child care social work. The decision-maker makes a final decision, after considering the recommendation of the fostering panel and, in some cases, the independent review panel.

Delegated authority

The Government sets out that authority for making day-to-day decisions for children and young people should be delegated to foster carers unless there is a good reason not to. This should be set out in the child's placement plan with the involvement of parents, the child or young person and the foster carer. Appropriate training and support should be provided.

Disclosure and Barring Service (DBS)

A national organisation conducting police checks to enable an assessment to be made on the suitability of a person to work with children. Different levels of check are available for different levels of regular contact and supervisory responsibility for children.

Exemption

An exemption from the usual fostering limit can be given by the area local authority where the foster carer lives, for a specific named child or children. General exemptions cannot be given.

Financial support in adoption

Adoption agencies can, in certain circumstances, pay a regular allowance to enable an adoption to go ahead which could not otherwise do so for financial reasons. This is not uncommon in cases where foster carers adopt a child in their care. It is reviewed annually.

Foster care agreement

Foster carers who are approved to care for children who are looked after by a local authority must complete an agreement with their approving agency that sets out the terms and conditions of their fostering role.

Fostering for Adoption

The Care Planning, Placement and Case Review (England) Regulations 2010 allow an agency to give an approved adopter temporary approval as a foster carer for a named child. This enables a child to be placed as a foster child with carers without them having had a full fostering assessment or been presented to the fostering panel. These will be children for whom the likelihood of eventual adoption is high. However, the child is fostered until, in most cases, work with birth parents and court involvement enables an adoption plan to be agreed and the child to be matched with these carers through the adoption panel process.

Fostering service provider

This includes both local authorities and independent agencies.

Independent fostering provider (IFP)

These are agencies that are not local authorities. They may be voluntary agencies, some of which may be registered charities, or they may be profit-making agencies.

Independent reviewing officer (IRO)

Chairs statutory child care reviews for looked after children. Chairs annual reviews of foster carers in some agencies.

Interim care order

An order made by a court giving a local authority the responsibility described above on an interim basis, pending a final decision by the court on whether or not to make a full care order.

Looked after

This term includes both children in care and accommodated children. Local authorities have certain duties towards all looked after children and their parents, which are set out in Part III of the Children Act 1989. These include the duty to safeguard and promote the child's welfare and the duty to consult with children and parents before taking decisions.

NMS

National Minimum Standards for Fostering Services 2011

Ofsted

The Office for Standards in Education. This body is responsible for the inspection and registration of all fostering services.

Open adoption

This term may be used very loosely and can mean anything from an adoption where a child continues to have frequent face-to-face contact with members of their birth family to an adoption where there is some degree of "openness", e.g. the birth family and adopters meeting each other once. People using the term should be asked to define what they mean!

Parental responsibility (PR)

This is defined in the Children Act 1989 as 'all the rights, duties, powers and responsibilities which by law a parent has in relation to a child and his property'. Other people may also have or acquire parental responsibility (see Conroy Harris, 2019, for full details). The most important elements of parental responsibility include providing a home for the child; having contact with the child; protecting and maintaining the child; disciplining the child; determining and providing for the child's education; determining the religion of the child; consenting to the child's medical treatment; and naming the child or agreeing to the child's change of name.

Placement plan

This plan sets out the responsibilities of a foster carer for the placement of an individual child. It may, for instance, spell out the contact arrangements for that child with their birth family. The plan should include the agreement for delegation of authority to the foster carer to make day-to-day decisions.

Placing authority

The local authority or voluntary organisation responsible for the child's placement.

Private fostering

Any child under 16, or 18 if the child is disabled, who lives continuously for 28 days or more with someone who is not a relative, is privately fostered. The child's parents make the placement and finance it. The child is not looked after by the local authority but the local authority must be notified of the arrangement.

Registered person

A person who either provides a fostering service (through an agency) and is registered to do so (the registered provider) or who manages the service and is registered to do so (the registered manager).

Registered provider

The registered provider of non-local authority fostering services may be an individual, a partnership or an organisation. If it is an organisation, it must name and register with Ofsted a "responsible individual" who is responsible for supervising the management of the fostering agency.

Responsible authority

The local authority that is looking after the child.

Special guardianship

An order under the Children Act 1989 offering an alternative legal status for children. The child is no longer looked after. It gives the special guardian parental responsibility which they can exercise to the exclusion of others. However, the birth parent(s) retain parental responsibility. Support services, including financial support, are very similar to those for adopters.

Supervising social worker (previously link worker)

This worker used to be called a link worker. They are the fostering team social worker who supervises and supports a foster carer.

Training, support and development standards

These provide a national benchmark that sets out what all foster carers should know, understand and be able to do within the first 12 months of approval (or 18 months for family and friends foster carers). There are seven standards: understand the principles and values essential for fostering children and young people; understand your role as a foster carer; understand health and safety and healthy caring; know how to communicate effectively; understand the development of children and young people; safeguard children and young people (keep them safe from harm); and develop yourself.

Useful organisations

CoramBAAF

**41 Brunswick Square
London WC1N 1AZ
Tel: 020 7520 0300
www.corambaaf.org.uk**

A membership organisation of agencies and individuals working to secure the best outcomes for looked after and adopted children.

Department for Education

Sanctuary Buildings
20 Great Smith Street
London SW1P 3BT
Tel: 0370 000 2288
www.education.gov.uk

Family Rights Group

The Print House
18 Ashwin Street
London E8 3DL
Tel: 0808 801 0366
Email: office@frg.org.uk
www.frg.org.uk

A national organisation that advises families who are in contact with children's services, about the care of their children.

Fostering Network

87 Blackfriars Road
London SE1 8HA
Tel: 020 7620 6400
Email: info@fostering.net
www.fostering.net

Produces a wide range of leaflets, publications and training materials on all aspects of foster care and a quarterly magazine. Offers advice and information on fostering.

Grandparents Plus

1 Addington Square
London SE5 0HF
Tel: 0300 123 7015
Email: advice@grandparentsplus.org.uk
www.grandparentsplus.org.uk

Offers advice and support to grandparents, and training for professionals who are working with grandparents who may be caring for their grandchildren.

Become (formerly Who Cares? Trust)

15–18 White Lion Street
London N1 9PG
Tel: 020 7251 3117
Email: advice@becomecharity.org.uk
www.becomecharity.org.uk/

Promotes services for children and young people in public care and those who have left public care.

Foster Talk

Oak Tree House
Waterside, Hanbury Road
Stoke Prior
Bromsgrove
B60 4FD
Tel: 01527 836910
www.fostertalk.org/

An organisation that provides independent support for foster carers in the UK.

Appendices

Forms available for purchase

The forms and sample documents are available here for agencies to copy, amend and use as they wish. All of these are also available as Word templates for purchase; the set costs £40.00 plus VAT for CoramBAAF members and £60.00 plus VAT for non-members. The package also includes CoramBAAF's pamphlets, *Thinking about Joining a Fostering Panel?* and *A Guide to Writing Panel Minutes.* These can be purchased, for unlimited future use, at: www.corambaaf.org.uk/bookshop, or by contacting CoramBAAF Publications Sales at pubs.sales@corambaaf.org.uk or on 020 7520 7517.

Appendix 1: Introduction to Fostering Services: National Minimum Standards 2011   63

Appendix 2: Training, Support and Development Standards   64

Appendix 3: Decision-making forms   66

Appendix 4: Job descriptions and person specifications for central list/panel members and panel Chair   70

Appendix 5: Interview questions for central list/panel members and panel Chair   74

Appendix 6: Code of conduct for panel members   75

Appendix 7: Review of central list/panel members   76

Appendix 8: Review of panel Chair   81

Appendix 9: Panel member notes sheet   87

Appendix 10: Quality of report   88

Appendix 11: Checklist of additional information that may be provided by the agency   90

Appendix 1
Introduction to Fostering Services: National Minimum Standards 2011

This document contains the National Minimum Standards (NMS) applicable to the provision of fostering services. The NMS, together with Regulations relevant to the placement of children in foster care, such as the Fostering Services (England) Regulations 2011 (the 2011 Regulations), form the basis of the regulatory framework under the Care Standards Act 2000 (CSA) for the conduct of fostering services.

The values statement below explains the important principles that underpin these standards.

Values

- The child's welfare, safety and needs are at the centre of their care.

- Children should have an enjoyable childhood, benefiting from excellent parenting and education, enjoying a wide range of opportunities to develop their talents and skills leading to a successful adult life.

- Children are entitled to grow up in a loving environment that can meet their developmental needs.

- Every child should have his or her wishes and feelings listened to and taken into account.

- Each child should be valued as an individual and given personalised support in line with their individual needs and background in order to develop their identity, self-confidence and self-worth.

- The particular needs of disabled children and children with complex needs will be fully recognised and taken into account.

- The significance of contact for looked after children, and of maintaining relationships with birth parents and the wider family, including siblings, half-siblings and grandparents, is recognised, as is the foster carer's role in this.

- Children in foster care deserve to be treated as a good parent would treat their own children and to have the opportunity for as full an experience of family life and childhood as possible, without unnecessary restrictions.

- The central importance of the child's relationship with their foster carer should be acknowledged and foster carers should be recognised as core members of the team working with the child.

- Foster carers have a right to full information about the child.

- It is essential that foster carers receive relevant support services and development opportunities in order to provide the best care for children.

- Genuine partnership between all those involved in fostering children is essential for the NMS to deliver the best outcomes for children; this includes the Government, local government, other statutory agencies, fostering service providers and foster carers.

(Reproduced from Fostering Services: National Minimum Standards 2011. This information is licensed under the terms of the Open Government Licence. Available at www.education.gov.uk.)

Appendix 2
Training, Support and Development Standards

It is expected that foster carers understand and can evidence that they meet the Training, Support and Development Standards within 12 months of their approval. The standards can be particularly helpful when considering reviews of foster carers and as a tool for decision-makers.

The standards are underpinned by certain principles and values, as set out below:

Principles and values

Principles

- The welfare of the child or young person is paramount.
- Carers contribute to children and young people's care, learning and development, and safeguarding. This is reflected in every aspect of practice and service provision.
- Carers support parents and families who are partners in the care, learning, development and safeguarding of their children, recognising they are the child or young person's first, and in most situations, their most enduring carers and educators.
- Carers are integral to the team supporting children and young people.

Values

- The needs, rights and views of the child or young person are at the centre of all practice and provision.
- Individuality, difference and diversity are valued and celebrated.
- Equality of opportunity and anti-discriminatory practice are actively promoted.
- Children and young people's health and well-being are actively promoted.
- Children and young people's personal and physical safety is safeguarded, whilst allowing for risk and challenge, as appropriate to the capabilities of the child or young person.
- Self-esteem and resilience are recognised as essential to every child and young person's development.
- Confidentiality and agreements about confidential information are respected as appropriate unless a child or young person's protection and well-being are at stake.
- Professional knowledge, skills and values are shared appropriately in order to enrich the experience of children and young people more widely.
- Social inclusion and advancement of children and young people are actively promoted as specified in the UN Convention on the Rights of the Child.

The Training, Support and Development Standards include:

Standard 1: Understand the principles and values essential for fostering children and young people

- The principles and values
- Equality, inclusion and anti-discriminatory practice
- Person-centred approaches
- Confidentiality and sharing information

Standard 2: Understand your role as a foster carer

- Fostering role
- Legislation, policies and procedures
- Relationships with parents and others
- Team working
- Being organised
- Complaints and compliments

Standard 3: Understand health and safety, and healthy care

- Legislation, policies and procedures
- Accommodation

- Healthy care and medication
- Personal safety and security
- Risk assessment

Standard 4: Know how to communicate effectively

- Encourage communication
- Knowing about communication
- Communication with parents, families and friends
- Communication with organisations
- Principles of keeping good records

Standard 5: Understand the development of children and young people

- Attachment and stages of development
- Resilience
- Transitions
- Supporting play, activities and learning
- Supporting educational potential
- Understanding contexts
- Promote positive sexual health and sexual identity
- Supporting disabled children and children with special emotional needs

Standard 6: Keep children and young people safe from harm

- Legislation, policies and procedures
- Keeping children safe
- Recognising and responding to abuse
- Working with other agencies
- "Whistleblowing"(reporting failures in duty)

Standard 7: Develop yourself

- Your role and approval as a foster carer
- Being aware of the impact of fostering on your sons and daughters and extended family
- Using support and supervision to develop your role
- Meeting learning needs as part of continuing professional development

(Reproduced from *Training, Support and Development Standards for Foster Carers: Guidance*, Department for Education, 2012)

NB For family and friends foster carers, they need to evidence that they understand and meet standards set out for them within 18 months of approval – see *Training, Support and Development Standards for Family and Friends Foster Carers: Supplementary guidance*, Department for Education, 2012. Foster carers who provide short breaks to disabled children and young people need to complete *Short Break Carers Training, Support and Development Standards* (Department for Education, 2012).

Appendix 3
Decision-making forms

Decision-makers may find the forms set out below helpful when making decisions or qualifying determinations about approvals of foster carers. All forms are fully compliant with case law, regulations and statutory guidance.

Stage 2 Decision Form (Approvals)

This sets out the process the decision-maker must follow when making decisions regarding suitability to foster at initial approval.

Decision Form (Reviews)

This sets out the process the decision-maker must follow when making decisions regarding suitability to foster following reviews (taken from CoramBAAF, 2019).

Qualifying Determination Form

This sets out the process the decision-maker must follow when making qualifying determinations regarding suitability to foster at initial approval and following reviews. It also includes changes or terminations of approval.

Stage 2 Decision Form (Approvals)

Name of applicant/s:

Date:

Name of decision-maker:

In making this decision, I have taken into account the following materials

Form F/PAR and panel minutes — YES/NO

Other material — YES/NO
If yes, please list:

Key considerations/arguments in this case

I agree with the process and approach of the assessment (including panel process), am satisfied as to its fairness, and satisfied that the arguments have been properly addressed — YES/NO

If no, provide details:

Recommendation of panel

This can be taken directly from panel minutes

Reasons given for this recommendation

These can be taken directly from panel minutes

I have considered additional material that was not available at panel — YES/NO

If yes, provide details of this information and how this has had an impact on the decision:

Decision

Reasons for decision

Please state the reasons you have adopted, by cross reference or otherwise, and any further reasons for your decision:

Advice to fostering service

Signed by decision-maker   **Date**

© CoramBAAF 2019

Reproduced from *Prospective Foster Carer Report (Form F) England* (CoramBAAF)

SAMPLE

Decision Form (Reviews)

Name of foster carer/s:

Date of review:

Date of panel (if applicable):

Name of decision-maker:

In making this decision, I have taken into account the following materials:

Foster carer review consisting of Forms FR	YES/NO
Fostering panel minutes	YES/NO/NA
Other material that was available at the time of the review *If yes, please list:*	YES/NO

Key considerations/arguments in this case

I agree with the process and approach of the review (including panel where applicable), am satisfied as to its fairness, and satisfied that the arguments have been properly addressed   YES/NO
If no, provide details:

Recommendation of fostering panel/fostering service
This can be taken directly from fostering panel minutes or from the fostering service manager report (FR-H)

Reasons given for this recommendation
These can be taken directly from fostering panel minutes or from the fostering service manager report (FR-H)

I have considered additional material that was not available at the time of the review (and panel if applicable)   YES/NO
If yes, provide details of this information and how this has had an impact on the decision:

Decision

Reasons for decision
Please state the reasons you have adopted, by cross reference or otherwise, and any further reasons for your decision:

Advice to fostering service

Signed by decision-maker   **Date**

© CoramBAAF 2019

SAMPLE

Qualifying Determination (QD) Form

Name of foster carer/s:

Date of review:

Date of panel (if applicable):

Name of decision-maker:

In making this qualifying determination, I have taken into account the following material

Form F/PAR, brief report, review paperwork and panel minutes	YES/NO
Other material *If yes, please list:*	YES/NO

Key considerations/arguments in this case

I agree with the process and approach of the assessment/review (including panel process), am satisfied as to its fairness, and satisfied that the arguments have been properly addressed — YES/NO

If no, provide details:

Recommendation of fostering panel/fostering service
This can be taken directly from fostering panel minutes or from the fostering service manager report

---

Reasons given for this recommendation
These can be taken directly from fostering panel minutes or from the fostering service manager report

---

I have considered additional material that was not available at panel or at the time of the review — YES/NO

If yes, provide details of this information and how this has had an impact on the qualifying determination:

Qualifying determination

Reasons for qualifying determination
Please state your reasons for making the qualifying determination:

Advice to fostering service

Signed by decision-maker   **Date**

© CoramBAAF 2019

Appendix 3

SAMPLE

Appendix 4
Job descriptions and person specifications for central list/panel members and panel Chair

Central list/panel members

Job description

1. To read the circulated papers carefully before the meeting and to attend the meeting prepared to raise issues and to contribute to the panel discussion.
2. To take responsibility for participating in the making of a recommendation, on each case, drawing on both personal and professional knowledge and experience.
3. To attend meetings of the panel as specified in your agreement with the agency.
4. To be prepared to attend additional panels if possible, if requested.
5. To participate, with other members, in advising on policy and procedural matters as required.
6. To address diversity issues and promote anti-discriminatory practice.
7. To safeguard the confidentiality of all panel papers and panel discussions.
8. To participate in induction and in training which will be at least one day per year.
9. To participate constructively in the annual review of your central list panel membership.
10. To adhere to the agency's panel member code of conduct, if provided (see Appendix 6).

Person specification

Experience and qualifications

- Experience, either professionally or personally or both, of the placement of children in foster families or of children being cared for away from their birth family.
- A social work qualification will be necessary for certain panel members.

Knowledge

- An appreciation of the effect of separation and loss on children.
- Awareness of the richness of different kinds of families and their potential for meeting children's needs.
- Some understanding of the purpose and function of the panel and of the agency which the panel is serving, or a willingness to learn.

Abilities

- Good listening and communication skills.
- The ability to read, process and analyse large amounts of complex and sometimes distressing information.
- The ability to make an assessment and to form a view, based on the written and verbal information presented to panel, and the confidence to articulate this at panel.
- The ability to use personal and/or professional knowledge and experience to contribute to discussions and decision-making in a balanced and informed manner.
- The ability to work co-operatively as part of a multi-disciplinary team.
- The ability to attend panel meetings, as required, arriving on time, and to attend at least one training day each year.

Attitudes

- A commitment to keeping children within their own family or community where this is possible and to maintaining contact between children living in foster families and their birth families where this appears to be in the child's best interests.
- A commitment to fostering as a way of meeting a child's needs where this appears to be in the child's best interests.
- A commitment to safeguarding and promoting children's welfare in foster care.
- A valuing of diversity in relation to issues of ethnicity, religion, gender, disability and sexuality.

- An understanding of, and a commitment to, the need for confidentiality.
- A willingness to increase knowledge and understanding of issues through reading, discussion and training.
- A willingness to contribute constructively to the annual review of your central list panel membership and, as required, to that of other members and the Chair.

SAMPLE

Panel Chair

Job description

1. To chair panel meetings, ensuring that all items of business are covered and that the panel operates in accordance with regulations and the policies and procedures of the agency.

2. To prepare for panel meetings, reading panel papers carefully, identifying key issues and alerting the agency adviser if necessary to ensure, as far as possible, that the case is adequate for submission to panel.

3. To facilitate the active participation of all panel members in contributing to the panel's consideration of cases and to the making of clear and well-evidenced recommendations with the reasons for these.

4. To ensure that all those attending panel are treated with respect and courtesy.

5. To address diversity issues and to promote anti-discriminatory practice at all times.

6. To ensure that clear and accurate minutes are written, which record any serious reservations which panel members may have, and to be involved in checking and agreeing draft minutes with other panel members before they are sent to the decision-maker.

7. To liaise with the decision-maker and with other senior managers as required.

8. To ensure, along with the agency adviser, that senior managers are aware of issues of concern, in relation both to individual cases and to more general matters.

9. To be involved in the recruitment and appointment of central list panel members and in any consideration about terminating the appointment of a member.

10. To review, possibly with the agency adviser, the performance of central list panel members as the need arises, and at least annually.

11. To assist in developing, promoting and monitoring policies and procedures and high standards of work in fostering services in the agency.

12. To assist in planning training for members and to participate in this at least one day per year.

13. To safeguard the confidentiality of all panel papers and panel discussions.

14. To be involved in:
    - deciding whether a case is adequate for submission to panel;
    - deciding on the attendance of observers at panel;
    - deciding on the participation of a panel member who declares an interest in a case;
    - deciding when an extra panel may be necessary;
    - the preparation of an annual report on the panel's work.

Person specification

Experience and qualifications

- Experience, either professionally or personally or both, of the placement of children in foster families and of children being cared for away from their birth family.
- Experience of chairing complex meetings.

Knowledge

- An appreciation of the effect of separation and loss on children.
- An awareness of the richness of different kinds of families and their potential for meeting children's needs.
- An understanding of the purpose and function of the panel and of the agency which the panel is serving.
- An understanding of the fostering process and practice and of the legislative framework for the work of the panel, or the capacity to develop this knowledge quickly.

Abilities

- The authority and competence to chair a panel, ensuring that the business is covered and that the panel operates in accordance with regulations and the policies and procedures of the agency.
- Excellent interpersonal and listening skills.

- The ability to communicate well and clearly both verbally and in writing.
- The ability to identify key issues and possible solutions and to communicate these clearly.
- The ability to facilitate the active participation of all panel members in contributing to the panel's consideration of cases and recommendations.
- The ability to manage the expression of strongly held but possibly conflicting views by panel members and to help the panel to reach a recommendation which takes account of all these views.
- The ability to take up issues as required with the agency, liaising with the decision-maker and other senior managers.
- The ability, working with the agency adviser, to review each panel member's performance when required, and at least annually, ensuring that this is a helpful and constructive process for both the panel member and the panel as a whole.

Attitudes

- A commitment to keeping children within their own family or community where this is possible and to maintaining contact between children living in foster families and their birth families where this appears to be in the child's best interests.
- A commitment to fostering as a way of meeting a child's needs, where this appears to be in the child's best interests.
- A commitment to safeguarding and promoting children's welfare in foster care.
- A valuing of diversity in relation to issues of ethnicity, religion, gender, disability and sexuality.
- An understanding of, and a commitment to, the need for confidentiality.
- A willingness to increase knowledge and understanding of issues through reading, discussion and training.
- A willingness to contribute constructively to the annual review of their role as panel Chair.

Appendix 5
Interview questions for central list/panel members and panel Chair

Central list/panel members

1. Can you highlight the key experiences and skills you would bring to the fostering panel?

2. As a panel member, what qualities would you be looking for to evidence that applicants would make a good foster carer?

3. Can you tell us about something you have read, seen or heard about relating to fostering or child care practice?

4. Foster carers come from many diverse backgrounds and family structures. What particular support needs might you want to consider for them?

5. What would you do if your views differed from those of the rest of the panel? Would you be able to share your views and challenge those of others?

6. How would you ensure that the voice of the child is brought into discussions at the fostering panel?

7. What do you think is the value of the fostering panel?

Panel Chair

1. Can you highlight the key experiences and skills you would bring to chairing the fostering panel?

2. What do you think has been a significant piece of fostering policy and/or legislation in the past five years?

3. How would you facilitate the active participation of all panel members in contributing to the panel's consideration of cases presented?

4. How, as Chair, would you manage disagreement between panel members in their analysis of the panel papers and recommendations to be made by the panel? Can you give an example?

5. What is your view on the relationship between the panel Chair, decision-maker and the agency? (Include the agency adviser where applicable.)

6. Can you give an example where you have addressed issues of diversity or discriminatory practice?

7. What do you see as your role in the oversight of panel minutes?

8. What do you see as the value of central list/panel members' annual reviews? Can you give an example of how you have used these to good effect?

SAMPLE

Appendix 6
Code of conduct for panel members

A code of conduct for panel members can be helpfully referred to when conducting central list/panel member annual reviews or if a member's behaviour needs addressing. A code of conduct could include the following:

- Panel members declare an interest and inform the Chair or agency prior to the panel meeting if the member has knowledge either personally or professionally of a case under consideration.

- Panel members read the papers in advance and come fully prepared to contribute to the panel meeting.

- Panel members inform the Chair or agency if they have any concerns about gaps in information in the paperwork prior to the panel meeting wherever possible.

- Panel members express their views in the panel meeting in an honest, straightforward and sensitive way.

- Panel members know that confidentiality is essential and comply with all data protection requirements.

- Panel members do not discuss the content of cases without all members being present in the meeting.

- Panel members are welcoming and courteous to other members and those presenting and are prepared to listen to and reflect on others' views.

- Panel members act in a non-discriminatory way and are willing to address equality and diversity issues.

- Panel members consider each case on its own merit and take responsibility for making their own evidence-based recommendations.

- Panel members arrive on time for panel meetings.

- Panel members check minutes carefully and respond in timeframes set.

- Panel members ensure that any paperwork is kept securely, and shredded or returned to the agency when the panel meeting is completed, and that any downloads (if permitted) on personal IT equipment are immediately deleted following the panel meeting.

- Panel members participate fully and constructively in the annual review of their performance as a central list member.

- Panel members inform the agency immediately if they have been charged, cautioned or convicted for any criminal offence or if any criminal proceedings are pending.

- Panel members inform the agency immediately of any professional disciplinary matters or of any significant changes of circumstances that may impact on their suitability to be a panel member.

Appendix 7
Review of central list/panel members

Introduction

An annual review of the performance of fostering panel and central list members is a regulatory requirement. (See Chapter 1 for more information.) This will be conducted by the Chair and possibly also by the agency adviser if there is one. An additional review can be convened, as required.

Preparation for the review (see sample forms overleaf)

- The member should complete a self-evaluation form.
- The agency adviser and/or Chair should prepare a summary of feedback made by presenting social workers, foster carers or other panel members.
- Both the member and the agency adviser should check and reflect on the issues in the member's panel agreement (see section in Chapter 1) and on the job description and person specification which the member has had. The code of conduct for panel members, if provided, should also be referred to.

At the review

The member, the Chair and the agency adviser should meet and should go through and discuss:

- the self-evaluation form;
- the summary of feedback;
- the panel agreement, and job description and person specification if applicable;
- the code of conduct for panel members, if used.

A written summary of the review should be made and signed by the member, the Chair and the agency adviser (if there is one) (see sample review form).

After the review

The written summary and the supporting documents should be kept on the member's personnel file.

SAMPLE

Form for obtaining feedback from agency staff for the annual review of central list/panel members

Please complete the questions below. These will be shared with panel members at their annual reviews.

1. What are the strengths of panel members, and are there things specific panel members do well?

2. What are the limitations of panel members and are there any concerns?

3. What works well at panel meetings?

4. What works less well and needs development?

Thank you. Your comments are very important and will assist in the development of the panel.

SAMPLE

Self-evaluation form for central list/panel member

Name:

For first year reviews, please answer questions 1 and 2 and then go to question 4 and complete all the following questions.

1. How have you found being a panel member and is it what you expected?

2. How did you find your induction? Is there anything outstanding?

For all other reviews, please start with question 3 and complete all the following questions.

3. How have you found being a panel member over the last year?

4. Have there been any significant events that have affected you over the last year? Do you feel these have had an impact on you as a panel member?

5. Over the last year, can you give an example of something of which you are really proud? (This can be from your personal or professional life or your work on the panel.)

6. What particular qualities, skills and knowledge have you developed or used in panel over the past year?

7. Can you think of a case at panel where you felt you could have done something differently or where you felt uncomfortable or upset? How was it managed and resolved?

SAMPLE

8. Do you feel able to raise views that differ from other panel members? Can you give an example? Do you feel your views are listened to?

9. How have you found the practical arrangements for panel over the year? For example, receiving paperwork, panel location, availability of refreshments?

10. Do you have any comments about the general functioning of the panel? In particular, how the panel processes work and whether you think that panel members understand their role within the code of conduct for panel members?

11. Do you get sufficient time to review the minutes and have you suggested any changes over the last year?

12. What training and development relevant to panel have you undertaken over the year? This could include training through your work or your own personal development.

13. What do you think your future training and development needs are?

14. Are you willing to continue on the central list over the next year?

Please note that you will be contacted separately for your views on the Chair's performance at the time of their review. (See sample form in Appendix 8.)

SAMPLE

Review for central list/panel member

Date:

Name:

Date of inclusion on the central list:

Date of panels invited to and attended in the last year:

Present at the review, e.g. panel member, Chair and agency adviser (if applicable)

1. In addition to their self-evaluation, what are the panel member's reflections on the last year? What has gone well? What have they found difficult? How have they developed as a panel member over the last year?

2. Describe any relevant feedback from people who have presented to panel and other panel members

3. Provide the views of the Chair and agency adviser to the panel (if applicable) regarding the panel member's performance. What has gone well? Are there any issues? What skills and knowledge have been demonstrated?

4. Is there anything that needs to change for the panel member, taking into account the agreed code of conduct for panel members or performance objectives?

5. Is there anything that needs to change in the way that panel processes work?

6. Training and development completed

7. Training and development needs for the next year

8. Action plan agreed, including who will do what and within what timescales

9. Agreed continued membership on the central list for the next year

SAMPLE

Appendix 8
Review of panel Chair

Introduction

A review of the performance of the panel Chair is a regulatory requirement. (See Chapter 1 for more information.) An additional review can be convened, as required, by the decision-maker or the panel Chair.

Preparation for the review (see sample forms overleaf)

- The panel Chair should complete a self-evaluation form (see overleaf).
- The agency adviser or decision-maker should prepare a summary of any feedback given by presenting social workers, foster carers or other panel members.
- Both the panel Chair and the decision-maker should check and reflect on the issues in the Chair's panel agreement (see section in Chapter 1) and on the job description and person specification which the Chair has had.

At the review

- The Chair and the decision-maker should meet to go through and discuss:
  - the self-evaluation form;
  - the summary of comments made;
  - the panel agreement, and job description and person specification if applicable.
- A written summary of the review should be made and signed by the Chair and the decision-maker (see sample form overleaf).

After the review

The written summary and the supporting documents should be kept on the Chair's personnel file.

SAMPLE

Form for obtaining feedback from agency staff and central list/panel members for the annual review of the panel Chair

Please complete the questions below. These will be shared with the panel Chair at their annual review.

1. What are the strengths of the panel Chair and what do they do well?

2. What are the limitations of the panel Chair and are there any concerns?

3. What works well at panel meetings?

4. What works less well and needs development?

Thank you. Your comments are very important and will assist in the review and development of the panel Chair.

SAMPLE

Self-evaluation form for panel Chair

Name:

For first year reviews, please answer questions 1 and 2 and then go to question 4 and complete all the following questions.

1. How have you found being a panel Chair over your first year and is it what you expected? What has helped you? What has hindered you?

2. How did you find your induction? Is there anything outstanding?

For all other reviews, please start with question 3 and complete all the following questions.

3. As panel Chair, how have you found your involvement with the agency over the last year?

4. Have there been any significant events that have affected you over the last year? Do you feel these have had an impact on you as panel Chair?

5. Over the last year, can you give an example of something of which you are really proud? (This can be from your personal or professional life or work on the panel.)

6. What particular qualities, skills and knowledge have you developed or used as panel Chair over the past year?

7. Can you think of a case at panel where you felt you could have done something differently or where you felt uncomfortable or upset? How was it managed and resolved?

8. Do you have an opportunity to receive peer support?

9. Can you give an example when there was conflict between panel members about a case or where there was conflict between the panel and the agency? How were matters resolved?

10. How do you think that panel is undertaking its quality assurance role? How does feedback to and from panel inform the work of the panel and the work of the agency?

11. How have you found the practical arrangements for panel over the year? For example, receiving paperwork, panel location, availability of refreshments?

12. Do you have any comments about the general functioning of the panel? In particular, how the panel processes work, including the signing off of minutes, and whether you think that panel members understand their role within the agreed code of conduct or their performance objectives?

13. What training and development relevant to panel and/or chairing have you undertaken over the year? This could include training through your work or your own personal development.

14. What do you think your future training and development needs are?

15. Are you willing to continue as panel Chair over the next year?

SAMPLE

Review for panel Chair

Date:

Name:

Date of inclusion on the central list:

Dates of panels invited to and attended in the last year:

Present at the review, e.g the Chair, decision-maker and agency adviser (if applicable):

1. In addition to their self-evaluation, what is the panel Chair's summary of reflections on the last year? What has gone well? What have they found difficult? How have they developed as panel Chair over the last year?

2. Describe relevant feedback from people who have presented to panel, other panel members and key agency staff

3. Provide the views of the decision-maker and agency adviser to the panel (if applicable) regarding the Chair's performance. What has gone well? Any issues? What skills and knowledge have been demonstrated?

4. What peer support is provided?

5. Is there anything that needs to change for the panel Chair, taking into account feedback and the job desciption and person specification?

6. Is there anything that needs to change in the way that panel processes work?

7. Training and development completed

8. Training and development needs for the next year

9. Action plan agreed, including who will do what and within what timescales

10. Agreement for the Chair to continue for the next year

NB Please attach written feedback from people who have presented to panel, panel members and agency staff.

SAMPLE

Appendix 9
Panel member notes sheet

Applicant/carer(s) name: *Use initials only*

Panel member's name:

Signature:

Date:

Purpose of presentation to panel:

Brief report, full assessment report or review

Strengths:

Concerns:

Questions:

Please leave panel member notes sheet with panel administrator following the panel meeting

SAMPLE

Appendix 10
Quality of report

Panel member's views

Send securely to the agency adviser if possible in advance of the fostering panel

Use initials of applicants/carers/SSWs to retain confidentiality

Initials of applicant/carer(s):

Initials of assessor/SSW:

Name of panel member:

Nature of report (i.e. full assessment/brief report/first review/other review/ assessment update):

Strengths of assessment – areas to consider:

- How clear a picture of the family/current circumstances does the paperwork provide?

- What degree of evidence is included that the applicants/carers understand the child's needs and have the skills necessary to help and support them?

- Are the reasons for the recommended terms of approval substantiated within the report in relation to age/type of fostering?

- Specify the depth/breadth/adequacy of information provided, degree of analysis, fluency of report writing, grammar and spelling

Concerns – areas to consider:

- Missing checks/gaps in information/lack of evidence/lack of clarity/poor presentation/out of timescales (maximum eight months for assessment, within period of one year for reviews)

- Grammar/spelling/errors (section/page)

Any other comments:

Adapted with permission from Fosterplus

SAMPLE

Panel Chair summary

(This summary will be provided to the assessing/supervising social worker for feedback on the quality of the report provided to the fostering panel, and collated for quarterly feedback to the fostering service on the quality of reports presented to the fostering panel.)

Name of applicant/carer(s):

Name of assessor/SSW:

Name of panel Chair completing summary:

Nature of report (i.e. full assessment/brief report/first review/other review/ assessment update):

Strengths of assessment:
As agreed by panel members prior to and at the panel meeting

Concerns:
As agreed by panel members prior to and at the panel meeting

Any other comments/overall rating of the quality of report:

Adapted with permission from Fosterplus

Appendix 11
Checklist of additional information that may be provided by the agency

Please tick if included

- [ ] List of central list members (with brief details and telephone numbers)
- [ ] Name, job title and telephone number of the agency adviser, if any
- [ ] Name and job title of the decision-maker(s)
- [ ] Central list panel member agreement for members
- [ ] Code of conduct for panel members
- [ ] Format for undertaking the annual review of central list panel members
- [ ] Statement of purpose for the fostering service
- [ ] The latest annual report of the panel, if one is produced
- [ ] The latest management report detailing activity levels in the agency's fostering work
- [ ] The latest set of policy and procedures for fostering work, including the panel's role and function
- [ ] The latest set of policy and procedures for family and friends/connected persons work
- [ ] Any other relevant policies not included in the above
- [ ] Arrangements for considering long-term fostering situations
- [ ] Information on the assessment and preparation process for applicants, including the programme for groups
- [ ] Complaints procedure
- [ ] Child care or permanence policy
- [ ] Safeguarding and child protection policy
- [ ] Children's guide
- [ ] Foster carer handbook
- [ ] Allowances paid to foster carers
- [ ] Privacy notice to comply with the GDPR
- [ ] Any other information

Books for your fostering service

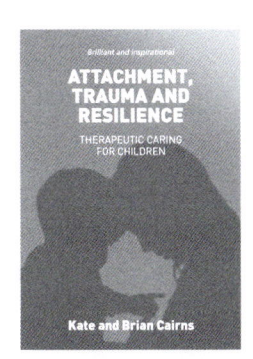

coramBAAF ADOPTION & FOSTERING ACADEMY

Attachment, trauma and resilience

A heartwarming book based on the authors' experience as social workers and foster carers of 12 children. It offers a vivid glimpse into life with children who have experienced attachment difficulties, loss and trauma, and shows how families can develop strategies to successfully handle a range of situations.

£15.95 — 2016

Attachment handbook for foster care and adoption

This comprehensive book provides an accessible account of core attachment concepts. It explains the dimensions of parenting associated with helping children to feel secure and to fulfil their potential in the family, with peers, at school and in the community.

£24.95 — 2018

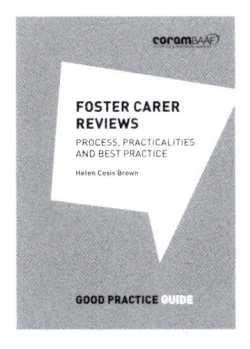

Foster carer reviews

Reviews of foster carers have a key role in evaluating foster care practice and improving the quality of foster care provided. This guide sets out the process and practicalities of conducting reviews and makes recommendations for good practice.

£12.95 — 2015

Parent and child fostering

This guide addresses the challenges faced by agencies and carers in parent and child fostering arrangements, focusing on the practical issues and amply illustrated with case examples of good practice. Offers valuable advice, information, and suggestions on how to deliver a good quality service.

£14.95 — 2011

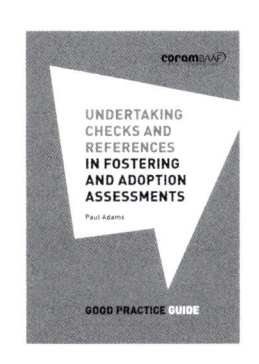

Undertaking Checks and References in Fostering and Adoption Assessments

This practice guide explores the various checks and references that can be undertaken by agencies during assessments, how best to undertake these, what information they will provide, and which checks are likely to be the most useful and effective.

£11.95 — 2017

Fostering Now

This pocket book provides a concise explanation of all the legislation relating to fostering in England. Ideal for all busy social work practitioners.

£8.95 — 2016

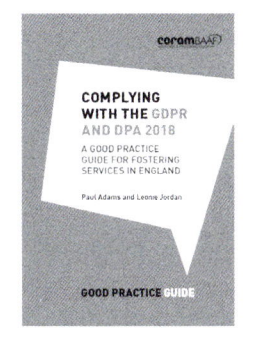

Complying with the GDPR and DPA 2018

This practice guide for fostering services in England explores and explains the GDPR and DPA 2018, and takes a practical approach to set out how fostering services can meet the requirements of this legislation.

£17.95 — 2019

The Secure Base Model

This guide and DVD for practitioners explores the Secure Base Model of caregiving, which uses a strengths-based approach to help make sense of looked after children's needs and behaviours.

£16.95 — 2014

How to run an effective panel!

Training for your panel members

Fostering and adoption panels lie at the very heart of our commitment to high quality family placement work. We offer a range of services to support the development of effective panels, including:

- **Regular workshops** exploring panel-related topics, all of them firmly placed in the context of the new statutory expectations:
  - being a member of a panel;
  - the agency adviser's role;
  - the panel administrator's role;
  - the role of the Chair;
  - effective agency decision-making.

- **Annual joint training day programmes**, specifically tailored programmes to meet your agency's needs, and enabling you to fulfil the expectations of the 2011 National Minimum Standards.

  Each person on the central list is given the opportunity of attending an annual joint training day with the fostering service's fostering/adoption staff.

  (Fostering NMS 23.10 and Adoption NMS 23.15)

- **Additional panel training** in relation to, for example, how panels should best consider assessments and reviews, how best to achieve robust quality assurance, or the panel's role in relation to allegation management and safeguarding issues.

- **Panel membership**. In addition to panel-related training, we also take on roles as panel members and panel Chairs. Our website is also a very effective way of recruiting a broad range of panel members.

For more information about any of these services please visit www.corambaaf.org.uk or contact tel. 020 7520 2046

coramBAAF
ADOPTION & FOSTERING ACADEMY

Advertise your panel vacancies on the CoramBAAF website

Our vacancies page is a great way to reach thousands of prospective panel members who specialise in fostering.

Attractive discounts are available for CoramBAAF members as well as reduced prices for multiple listings.

All vacancies are also included in our weekly job vacancies e-newsletter.

To find out more, visit
www.corambaaf.org.uk/jobs
or contact the Jobs Listings team at
jobslistings@corambaaf.org.uk

CoramBAAF
ADOPTION & FOSTERING ACADEMY

Registered as a company limited by guarantee in England and Wales No. 9697712. Part of the Coram Group. Charity No. 312278. Registered Office at 41 Brunswick Square, London WC1N 1AZ.